Invisible Capitalism

Invisible Capitalism

Beyond Monetary Economy
and the Birth of New Paradigm Economies

Hiroshi Tasaka

Jorge Pinto Books Inc.
New York

This English edition is published in 2009 by Jorge Pinto Books Inc., 151 East 58th Street, New York, New York, 10022, U.S.A. under permission of and by arrangement with the author.

This book was originally published in Japanese under the title

"目に見えない資本主義"

by Toyo Keizai, Inc. Tokyo, Japan in 2009.

Original cover design : Kiyoshi Ishima
Cover design : Susan Hildebrand
Translation : Babel Corporation, website : www.babeltmc.com

ISBN: 1-934978-27-2
978-1-934978-27-6

This edition of *Invisible Capitalism* is published under the Books in Translation series of Jorge Pinto Books Inc.

How can we foresee the future of capitalism?

By taking off old glasses.

The old glasses of "monetary economy."

Contents

Preface

The Capitalism of 21st Century
Will Move toward the Capitalism
That Emphasizes "Invisible Capital"

Which path will capitalism be taking from now?

As we have been experiencing the global economic crisis triggered by global capitalism, this must be the question that many people around the world hold in their minds now.

And concurrently, many people are feeling that capitalism must overcome this crisis and mature toward the future.

Then, what is "maturity" of capitalism?

In order to know the answer to this, we should ask this question:

What is "maturity" of the human mind?

The answer to this question is clear.

To become able to see "invisible values."

That is, as the human mind develops and matures, it becomes able to see "invisible values."

Such as "wisdom inexpressible in words," "human relationships through sympathy," "trust between humans," "reputation in the world," "cultures of organizations or societies," and so forth.

It becomes able to see these "invisible values."
This is what "maturity" of the human mind means.

If so, what is "maturity" of capitalism?

The answer to this question is also clear.

For capitalism
to become the capitalism that emphasizes "invisible capital."

This is precisely what maturity of capitalism means.

Then, how can we realize this maturity of capitalism?

By taking off our old glasses and looking around.

The old glasses of "monetary economy."

If we take off these glasses and look around, we become able to see how capitalism will mature toward the future.

Up until now, amid the overwhelming influence of global capitalism, our eyes have been caught in the "visible capital" called "money." We therefore have failed to truly turn our eyes to "invisible capital."

However, the fact that global capitalism has hit a wall through the experience of the global economic crisis is, in a sense, a good opportunity for capitalism to evolve toward a more mature stage.

And, once we take off the glasses called "monetary economy" and look around, we are able to see that great paradigm shifts are occurring in the economic principles that underlie capitalism.

Those are the "five paradigm shifts", as described below.

(1) The paradigm shift from "operationalism economy" to "complexity economy."
(2) The paradigm shift from "knowledge economy" to "empathy economy."
(3) The paradigm shift from "monetary economy" to "voluntary economy."
(4) The paradigm shift from "beneficiary economy" to "participatory economy."
(5) The paradigm shift from "unlimited growth economy" to "global environment economy."

And, all of these five paradigm shifts are precisely the shifts to the economic principles that go beyond "monetary economy." In other words, all of these paradigm shifts are the shift from "visible economy" to "invisible economy."

Then, what are the "new value systems" that will be required of us in these paradigms of "new economic principles"?

When we think about this, we realize something strange.

We realize that these "new economic principles" are in fact "nostalgic economic principles," and that the "new value systems" are in fact "nostalgic value systems."
In other words, we realize that so-called "new economic principles" are those that used to exist in every nation and in any region, and that so-called "new value systems" are those that used to exist in every nation and in any region.

Then why does such a strange thing happen?

That is because history goes through "dialectic development."

Dialectic is known as the philosophy of the German Idealist

philosopher Georg Hegel, and it includes the idea referred to as the "law of spiral development."

This law means that the world we live in develops as if it were climbing up a spiral staircase.

That is, just as people going up a spiral staircase, when looked at from above, will go around and return to the original place, old and nostalgic things revive as the world develops. But, since this is a spiral staircase, the world does not simply return to the same place as before; it invariably attains one level higher.

In other words, when the world progresses, develops, and evolves, there is invariably a revival of "old and nostalgic things." But each revival is accompanied by "new values."

This is the "law of spiral development."

And this is the reason that the regression to "nostalgic economic principles" through the "five paradigm shifts" of economic principles underlying capitalism will occur. Also, the reason that the value systems which are required of us will regress to "nostalgic value systems."

However, this will not be a simple "regression." This will not be a simple "revival."

The "regression," and the "revival," will invariably be accompanied by "new values."

Then, what are those "five paradigm shifts" that are about to occur in economic principles?

What are the "nostalgic economic principles" that will revive as a consequence of those paradigm shifts?

And what are the "nostalgic value systems" that will be required of us from now on?

In what way will those value systems be different from the "old value systems" of the past?

What kinds of "new values" will be added?

In this book, I will be discussing this subject with the focus on "the capitalism of Japan."

However, the contents provided in this book will presumably be informative not only to Japanese people but also to the people in many other nations.

Because, the "five paradigm shifts of economic principles" that are discussed in this book will definitely occur in every nation in the world.

And, in every nation, "nostalgic value systems" will definitely revive as the nation's capitalism matures.

Therefore, I thought that this book should be published not only in Japanese but also in English at the same time so that many people around the world may read it.

In the nation of Japan, we aim for the "capitalism that emphasizes invisible capital," namely, "invisible capitalism" toward the future. This vision of "invisible capitalism" will be informative to many people around the world who are now working to, amid this strong tide of global capitalism, create "mature capitalism" based on each nation's or region's own history, traditions, and culture.

If this book becomes one that gives new insights and courage to all the people who make an effort to change the capitalism through their daily work, seeking to realize the "more mature capitalism," the "more diverse capitalism," and the "more humane capitalism" that go beyond the limitation of global capitalism focused only on "visible capital" and "visible values," I, as the author, will be most delighted.

Hiroshi Tasaka

Chapter 1

What Will Happen

in the Future of Capitalism?

The Global Economic Crisis

Caused by "Global Capitalism"

What will happen in the future of capitalism?

In the midst of the unprecedented economic crisis that is affecting the entire globe, this must be the question that everyone holds in their minds now.

I have written this book to answer this question.

Actually, it was at an international conference I attended back in January 2009 when I felt it necessary to write this book.

The 2009 meeting of the World Economic Forum (WEF), known as the Davos Conference.

This annual meeting held in January in Davos, Switzerland gathers many influential people from all over the world—well-known politicians, executives, economists, and other intellects—for discussions on various issues that the world is faced with. Since the 2009 Davos Conference met in the midst of the global economic crisis, it attracted more attention globally than any other year in its thirty-eight-year history.

As I was a member of the Global Agenda Council of WEF, I attended this 2009 Conference and had the opportunity to join various sessions to listen to what attendees spoke on key issues.

Just like any other year, the heads of states of different nations, including Prime Minister Vladimir Putin of Russia, Prime Minister Wen Jiabao of China, Chancellor Angela Merkel of Germany, Prime Minister Gordon Brown and former Prime Minister Tony Blair of the United Kingdom, and former President Bill Clinton and former Vice President Albert Gore of the United States, among others, spoke on the platform at plenary sessions.

Eminent economists and other intellects as well, including a winner of the Nobel Prize in Economic Science Joseph Stiglitz and Nobel Peace Prize winner Muhammad Yunus, participated in different sessions and earnestly expressed their views on each topic.

Many of those discussions were naturally focused on the ways in which the current economic crisis could be resolved. Participants sometimes had heated discussions and other times spoke in unison on such issues as coordinated international actions, government financial intervention, preservation of free market, fiscal spending, and economic stimulus programs.

Needless to say, all of those discussions were of great importance in the sense that they dealt with the most urgent subject: the course of action to cope with the global economic crisis. And, every one of the participants who joined the discussions, whether politician, executive, economist, or intellect, was seriously and earnestly presenting their opinions about the measures required for this crisis. However, to be honest, I was not able to hear much of the kind of discussions I was secretly hoping for.

What will happen in the future of capitalism?

This is what I really wished to hear.

In such a situation, I was profoundly impressed by a speech presented by one particular participant at a plenary session.

His speech did not provide an answer to my question, but I felt that his opinion most precisely pointed out the essence of the current global economic crisis.

Interestingly enough, that speaker was neither a famous politician nor a renowned economist.

He was a religious leader.

His name was Jim Wallis, a minister of a Christian church in the United States.

At a panel discussion with such people as the U.K.'s former Prime Minister Tony Blair and Israel's President Shimon Peres, he presented the following view:

> When I turn on the TV every morning, CNN is there
> and they always talk about this same question:
>   "How long will this crisis last?"
> But I don't believe that is the right question to ask.
> What I believe we should be asking is different.
>   "How will this crisis change us?"
> That is what we should be asking.
> This crisis will eventually see its end.
> However, if we don't change our ways of doing
> business by the time it is all over, the pain and
> suffering that many people experience during the
> crisis will all be in vain.

I believe he is absolutely correct.

For sure, in the face of the current global recession that worsens rapidly, it is extremely meaningful that the leaders of different nations get together and discuss various kinds of emergency measures to mitigate the situation.

Any one of the earlier-mentioned issues—coordinated international actions, government financial intervention, preservation of free market, fiscal spending, and economic stimulus programs—will require a long time just to bridge the gaps in each nation's policies and require an even longer time to gain international consensus. It goes without saying that it is of great importance to discuss thoroughly in such an international conference setting as the Davos Conference.

However, here is one thing that we should realize:

"Relieving symptoms" and "curing illnesses" are fundamentally two very different things.

We should realize this fact.

If we think in terms of illnesses, for instance, acute symptoms such as high fever and bleeding should first be mitigated by immediately applying appropriate treatments, otherwise they could be fatal. However, relief of symptoms through symptomatic treatments is not equal to the complete cure of the illness.

A wise doctor who knows how to truly cope with illnesses would not only try to apply symptomatic treatments to relieve acute symptoms but also diagnose the underlying cause of the illness and consider holistic treatments including the improvements in health and lifestyle of patients. If the doctor has profound wisdom, he or she clearly knows what it really means to cure illnesses:

"Curing illnesses" does not simply mean "recovering health" but it does mean the "evolution of living system."

In other words, recovering from illnesses does not simply mean recovering health and going back to the original state. Through falling ill, we experience evolution at different levels of our living systems, such as body, lifestyle, and awareness. Through falling ill, various evolutions occur—our immune systems will be reinforced, our rhythm of daily life will be more natural, and our awareness will become more harmonious with our surroundings.

Such subtleties are concisely expressed in an old saying on illnesses:

"Illness conveys enlightenment."

This is true. Illnesses are not just "unfortunate events." They can provide us with a "good opportunity" to reflect deeply on how we should be, to change our lifestyle, to improve our health, and to heighten our awareness. This is what the saying teaches us.

And, this wisdom on illnesses also directly teaches us how the wisdom to cope with the current global economic crisis should be.

Why did this economic crisis happen?

The crisis is not just an "unfortunate event."

It provides us with a "good opportunity" to reflect deeply on the current capitalism of the world, to change political and economic systems, and to create new value systems and cultures in our society.

However, in order to turn this global economic crisis into a "good opportunity" without passing it over as a mere "unfortunate event," we should not be focusing only on "relieving the symptoms" of the "illness called economic crisis," but we must ultimately be aiming for the "cure of the illness." More specifically, we should not just be aiming for "recovering health" but for the "cure" that involves the "evolution of living systems."

The "New Capitalism" Which Will Be Born beyond the Global Economic Crisis

Actually, this is a fact that many people around the world are already aware of.

Many people throughout the world, as they experienced the outbreak of this global economic crisis, actually thought in their minds:

"I had a feeling that this sort of collapse would happen someday."

For sure, many people thought so in their minds.

In fact, when we reflect on these past few decades, we have witnessed the way that financial capitalism generated profits in "alchemical" manners as it made full use of state-of-the-art technology of "financial engineering," and anybody with ordinary senses felt inside that "Something does not seem right." However, since ordinary people did not have enough knowledge to discuss financial products like derivatives that involved high-level mathematical concepts nor enough wisdom to refute the theories presented by Nobel Prize-winning economists, they could only say to themselves that "But still, something does not seem right" when they were asked "What do you think is wrong?"

So, many people around the world thought in their minds:

"I had a feeling that this sort of collapse would happen someday."

And now, there is another concern that many people around the world feel in their hearts.

What is it?

"The world may not learn anything meaningful through this crisis."

This is the concern they have.

It is because many people are afraid that the measures for the current global economic crisis focus only on "symptomatic treatments."

In the world of modern medicine, ironically, the most advanced doctors with the highest level of knowledge and techniques tend to focus only on "relieving symptoms" and "symptomatic treatments" and tend to be oblivious to "curing illnesses," the true purpose. Similarly with regard to the economic world, many people are

7

concerned about the possibility that economists and administrative officials with the highest level of knowledge and techniques may fall into the same tendency. And, it was not a politician nor an economist, but a religious leader who was able to keenly and precisely sense what people were really feeling inside and express that thought in words.

So, we must be aware of the following.

As Jim Wallis said, this crisis will eventually come to an end. However, we are now presented with a fundamental problem that cannot be concluded with comments such as "Wall Street active again" or "The global economy on its way to recovery" when this crisis ends.

Because, this global economic crisis is not just a matter of "bad loans" nor "credit meltdown."

It is an essential crisis existing within the current so-called "global capitalism." And if we focus only on various symptomatic treatments without deeply questioning the fundamental problems of global capitalism, we will not be able to learn anything meaningful from this crisis and will end up with the same problem someday.

Considering the magnitude of the current global economic crisis, the world is expected to experience the "winter years" for a certain period of time to come.

If so, what we need to deeply consider is how capitalism should change beyond the coming "winter years."

Even during the extreme cold of winter, trees steadily nurture "new buds" under the bark.

And once winter is over, those buds start to flower dynamically.

When we apply this metaphor to capitalism, what would be the "new buds" that we should be nurturing now?

What kind of capitalism will come next?

What kind of evolution, unlike conventional capitalism, will the new capitalism have gone through?

These are what we should be discussing.

Why Has not Conventional Economics Discussed the "Evolution of Capitalism"?

Now, readers may have this question in mind:

"I understand that capitalism needs to be evolved.
However, aren't many economists already aware of that?
Then why isn't the 'evolution of capitalism' discussed that much?
Why hasn't the 'evolution of capitalism' been discussed in conventional economics?"

This is certainly true.
For instance, regarding the Davos Conference mentioned earlier. Even at such a setting, where a number of eminent economists gathered from around the world, the "evolution of capitalism" was not discussed that much.
What is the reason for this?
Actually, the reason is quite simple:

The "evolution of capitalism" is occurring beyond the "realm" of conventional economics.

Then, what is the "realm" of conventional economics?

It is "monetary economy."

In conventional economics, whether Keynesian or monetarist, we have always discussed markets, economies and capitalism within the realm of "monetary economy." In other words, we have always discussed capitalism in the paradigm (basic framework) of "monetary economy."

However, the "evolution of capitalism" that is occurring today is actually triggered by the shifts of the paradigm itself. This evolution is caused by the fact that the "economic principles" underlying current capitalism are evolving into new principles beyond the conventional monetary economy.

Nevertheless, conventional economics always interprets all the current events in capitalist societies from the viewpoint of "monetary economy." Therefore, it is not able to see the paradigm shifts that are occurring in the "economic principles," and thus it cannot see the evolution of "capitalism" as well.

That is precisely the reason that we cannot discuss the "evolution of capitalism" within the realm of conventional economics.

"We cannot see the new world with old glasses."

As this proverb suggests, so long as we are looking at the world, societies and economies within the paradigm of "monetary economy," there exists what we cannot see. Therefore we need to take off our glasses called "monetary economy" and look into the paradigm shifts of economic principles as well as the evolution of capitalism that are occurring now.

Otherwise we will end up with one of the following: We will not be able to understand the events that are happening beyond the "monetary economy" paradigm, we will not even try to understand them, or we will wrongly understand them within the paradigm of "monetary economy."

That is precisely why conventional economics has not discussed much about the "evolution of capitalism."

Then, what are the economic principles beyond the "monetary economy" paradigm?

Do such principles actually exist?

The answer can be found easily if we take a broad look at our past, not on the scale of capitalism's history but on the scale of human history as a whole.

For instance, what existed before "monetary economy" was born in human history?

"Barter economy."

It is an economy where people exchange goods without the use of money.

Then, what existed before "barter economy" was born?

"Gift economy."

It is an economy where people give goods to others through goodwill and affection.

Now, are "barter economy" and "gift economy" extinct forms of economy that had been long gone in the past?

The answer is, no.

We will discuss the meaning of this in detail later in this book.

However, in order to discuss the paradigm shifts in economic principles as well as the evolution of capitalism, there is one thing that is required of us:

To broaden our perspective.

That is because, in order to discuss the future of capitalism today, we need a wide range of interdisciplinary viewpoints, not limited to those of economists but of philosophy, history, cultural anthropology, religious studies, politics, sociology, business administration, psychology, information science, and more.

I have written this book to foster this discussion.

In this book, we will discuss the future of capitalism from a wide range of perspectives, which go beyond "monetary economy."

And then, we will discuss what the capitalism of Japan should aim for toward the future, and what will happen in so-called

Japanese style management in the future.

What kind of evolution will occur in capitalism from now?
And what kind of paradigm shifts in "economic principles" is it
that will promote the evolution?
We will begin with these subjects.

The Five Paradigm Shifts Which Will Occur

in the "Economic Principle" of Capitalism

First, I will present the conclusion here.
From now, great paradigm shifts will occur in the "economic
principles" that underlie capitalism.

Those are the "five paradigm shifts," as described below.

The first paradigm shift:
from "operationalism economy" to "complexity economy"

The second paradigm shift:
from "knowledge economy" to "empathy economy"

The third paradigm shift:
from "monetary economy" to "voluntary economy"

The fourth paradigm shift:
from "beneficiary economy" to "participatory economy"

The fifth paradigm shift:
from "unlimited growth economy"
to "global environment economy"

These "five paradigm shifts" will promote the evolution of capitalism from now.

And, all of these paradigm shifts will occur beyond the paradigm of "monetary economy" that has been the basis of conventional economics.

At the same time, the "five paradigm shifts" are none other than the "five aspects" of the fundamental paradigm shift that will occur in economic principles.

Then what kind of paradigm shift is it?

It is the paradigm shift from "visible economy" to "invisible economy."

And that will promote the evolution of capitalism in the future.

From "visible capitalism" to "invisible capitalism."

That paradigm shift will promote this evolution.

To illustrate the "vision of the evolution of capitalism" is one of the purposes of this book.

Then, why will those "five paradigm shifts" occur in the economic principles in the future?

We will discuss this subject first.

Chapter 2

The Philosophy to Foresee

the Future of Capitalism

How Can We Foresee the Future?

Before entering into this subject, there is one topic that needs to be considered.

How can we foresee the future?

The method for this should be discussed.
Because, discussing what kinds of paradigm shifts will occur in economic principles and in what direction capitalism will evolve in the future is precisely the same as foreseeing the future.

Then, how can we foresee the future?
Now, please take notice of this:
I am suggesting that we "foresee the future," not "predict the future."
Why is this?

Because we cannot "predict" the future.

In the present time, we cannot make concrete or quantitative predictions about the future.
There are three reasons for this.

The first reason is "discontinuity."

Most of the changes that will happen in the coming age will not be "continuous" ones. They will be "discontinuous" and "dramatic" changes that are cut from the past. The future will arrive all of a sudden, with no relation to the past. That must be why in the present time the word "evolution" is often preferred over the word "change." In the age of "discontinuity" like this, we cannot see the future just by investigating and analyzing "past tendencies." In addition, we cannot predict the future based on "past changes."

The second reason is "non-linearity."

In a highly-complex society, economy, or market, a "slight fluctuation" born at the corner of these systems can eventually cause "enormous changes" in the entire systems. It is the so-called "butterfly effect." The phenomenon can be described as this: "When a butterfly flutters its wings in Beijing, a hurricane occurs in New York." In other words, "slight fluctuations" in the present can bring about "enormous changes" in the future. Therefore, if we just look at "current major trends," we cannot know the future.

The third reason is "acceleration."

We have entered the "dog year" age, when the changes that took seven years to develop in the past now take place in only one year. Or perhaps it is the "mouse year" age, when the changes that took eighteen years in the past can take place in just one year. Changes of all things and beings are now accelerated. In such an age, when we predict the future, the future has already gone by. Therefore, if we think only of "changes in the near future," we actually cannot see the future itself.

"Discontinuity," "non-linearity" and "acceleration."

These three factors are what make "predicting the future" extremely difficult in the present time.

Then, what should we do?

If the future cannot be "predicted," what should we do?

The answer to this question was suggested at the beginning of this chapter.

We cannot "predict" the future.
But we can "foresee" it.

We cannot predict "specific changes."
But we can foresee "macroscopic trends."

We cannot make "concrete predictions" or "quantitative predictions" such as "This will happen within so many years" or "The scale of this will be approximately this much." But we can make "macroscopic foreseeing" or "directional foreseeing" such as "These kinds of trends will appear in society" or "The world will move in this direction."

We cannot predict the "detailed changes" that will happen in the future. However, we can foresee the "major trends" that will occur in the future.

For instance, we make a sand pile on the beach. Then we pour water on top. What course does the water take as it flows down the sand pile? It is affected by chance and fluctuation, so nobody can predict it. However, there is one thing we know for certain:

Water will always flow toward a lower level.

This is the essence of what we call a "macro view."

And, by employing this "macro view," we can "foresee" the future.

If so, how can we acquire this "macro view"?

By learning the "laws" of world development.

This is what is required of us.

The "world" in this context means all things and beings, including nature, society and human beings.

How does the "world" change, develop and evolve?

We are required to learn the "laws" that explain this.

If so, how can we learn these laws of world development?

Through "philosophy."

By studying philosophy, we are able to learn the "laws" of world development.

Because, "philosophy" is fundamentally a way to discern the "basic nature" of the world as well as the "laws" that lie at the basis of world change, development and evolution.

If so, what kind of specific philosophy is this?

It is "dialectic."

The philosophy of dialectic teaches us the "laws" of the changes, development and evolution of the world.

Then, what kind of philosophy is this "dialectic"?

The Future of Capitalism

Foreseen by "Dialectic"

When hearing the word "dialectic," the person that immediately comes to many readers' minds must be Georg Hegel, a German Idealist philosopher.

However, the philosophy of dialectic does not belong only to Hegel. In the history of Western philosophy, it was originated in the ancient times of Socrates and has been discussed by many philosophers until the modern times of Jean-Paul Sartre. In Eastern philosophy as well, it has been discussed in various teachings such as Buddhism, esoteric Buddhism, Taoism, Zen, and so forth.

And then, when these two key words "capitalism" and "dialectic" are raised, the person that comes to many readers' minds must be the German philosopher Karl Marx.

He developed the Dialectic of Hegel further and formulated the philosophy of Dialectical Materialism. By applying this philosophy, he wrote many works including *Capital: A Critique of Political Economy* and foresaw the future of capitalism. Therefore, it is no exaggeration to say that all of Marx's insights that underlie his prolific works are based on dialectic thinking.

However, in response to the statement "Marx foresaw the future of capitalism," some readers may present this question: "Marx was an active leader of capitalism criticism and a symbol of anti-capitalistic thought, wasn't he?"

But if we deeply interpret Marx's thought, we will understand that his thought was not just a simple "criticism of capitalism" nor "anti-capitalistic." Rather, among many philosophers he was one of the few who deeply understood, and had keen insight into, the dialectic dynamism of capitalism and of monetary economy. Many of his insightful thoughts are worth studying even in the present time, which is especially true with his theories of "the alienation of labor" and "monetary fetishism," as well as with his "revolution in developed nations" where he stated that "New social systems will emerge from inside a fully-developed capitalism."

For instance, his theory of "the alienation of labor."

Marx stated that the notion of "labor," which in its essence should be a joy for human beings, had been transformed into a "commodity" with the arrival of monetary economy and therefore the joy of labor had been lost. Thus, "labor" had turned into something remote that was "alienated" from human beings. In the present age, when the words "joy of working" are lost in the workplace, this insight of Marx should be reconsidered in depth.

Another instance is his theory of "monetary fetishism."

"Money" was an extremely useful medium which could equally and objectively measure the exchange value of various commodities flooding in the world, so it had brought about highly-advanced capitalism. On the other hand, it gave people the illusion that any commodities could be obtained as long as they acquired money, and moreover, the illusion that all the values in the world could be made into commodities. Consequently, it gave the even further illusion that money was the "Almighty" beyond the simple meaning of a "useful medium," thus "monetary fetishism" was created. This insight of Marx is also a thought we should open-mindedly learn from in this age when worship of money prevails.

Yet another instance is his theory of "revolution in developed nations."

New social systems that transcend capitalism would inevitably be born from inside a fully-developed and mature capitalism. Although this insight of his was not realized in the form of "socialist revolution as a result of class struggle between workers and capitalists" as he had foreseen, this is also a thought to be deeply reconsidered, in this age when the "evolution of capitalism" is about to occur through the dynamism of capitalism as living system.

In my youth, having a desire to find out the future of humankind, I read a number of writings in pursuit of visions and ideas about it. There were many of Marx's works among those writings, and one of the ideas in his works that particularly impressed me was his insight into "dialectic dynamism" of capitalism and of monetary economy.

When we reconsider his thoughts now in this age when capitalism has developed to the stage of "global capitalism," we find that he made several very striking points in his insights into the essential problems of capitalism as well as in his vision into the future of capitalism.

In a sense, the points he made seem to have foreseen the future of capitalism more precisely than the views of other economists and sociologists who consider capitalism only within the framework of the thought of capitalism.

The intellectual method that Karl Marx applied in foreseeing the future of capitalism was the philosophy of "dialectic."

However, any thought, no matter how insightful, is inevitably subject to the constraint of various historical factors. In this sense, the historical factors that did not exist in Marx's time, such as the "Internet revolution," the "global environmental problems" and the "emergence of complexity society" in particular, require us new insights into the future of capitalism.

For instance, the "Internet revolution."

This revolution enabled many people to freely share and utilize the information that exists in society, to create new knowledge and wisdom, and to take on collaborative actions at a global level. Such social situation did not exist in the time of Marx.

Another instance is the "global environmental problems."

Through these problems, it has become a clear and common understanding that people throughout the world, regardless of nation or ethnicity, are connected with each other by interests common to all humankind. It has also become a common understanding that economic growth of humankind as a whole will be "limited growth" within the constraint of "limited space" and "limited resources." Such situation did not exist either in Marx's time.

And finally, the "emergence of complexity society."

As societies increased in complexity, the social form that can be called "complexity society" has emerged. Consequently, societies have evolved into the kind of systems where it is extremely difficult for governments to politically manage and lead. Such situation did not exist either in Marx's time.

Interestingly, in the present time, if we work to foresee the future of capitalism through taking into account those new historical factors as well as applying this dialectic thinking, we are able to see various future scenarios that have not been discussed in the realm of conventional economics. In addition, we are able to see scenarios of future capitalism and human society that could not have been foreseen in Marx's time.

One of the purposes of this book is to discuss the future that Marx could not foresee.

Then, what kind of philosophy is this "dialectic"?

Dialectic is the philosophy that explains the changes, development and evolution of the world, and in short, there are "five laws" in dialectic. Considering the limited amount of space in this book, however, I will outline the "three laws," which are the most useful of the five in foreseeing the future of capitalism.

Readers who are interested in the philosophy of dialectic and in foreseeing the future by applying dialectic may refer to my other publication *The Five Laws to Foresee the Future: 12 Paradigm Shifts That Will Happen in the Future of Human Society* (Jorge Pinto Books Inc.).

The World Develops as if It Were Climbing a "Spiral Staircase"

Then, what is the first law of dialectic?

It is the "law of spiral development."

This law means that "The world develops as if it were climbing a spiral staircase."

It is often misunderstood that "The world develops upward in a straight line" and that "The world develops through the process in which old things disappear and new things are born."

In truth, the world develops as if it were climbing a spiral staircase. To illustrate this more clearly, let us imagine people going up a spiral staircase. When looked at from the side, they are climbing higher, or in other words, progressing and developing. However, when looked at from above, the people are going around the staircase and returning to their original place, which can be viewed as a revival or restoration. But, they are not simply at the original place; they are in fact at one level higher each time a circuit is completed. There is invariably a certain progress each time.

That is, in the development of the world, old and nostalgic things revive as the world develops. However, this is not a simple revival; it is a revival of old things that are accompanied by "new values."

In other words, this law means that the "evolution to the future" and the "regression to the origin" occur simultaneously.

This is the "law of spiral development."

Then, what are specific instances of the law?

In this modern age there are countless cases of it.

For instance, the Net "auction" and "reverse auction," which are receiving a lot of attention as the most advanced business model in the Internet world today.

They are, as a matter of fact, the revival of "bidding method" and "limit price method," which in the old days were common practices in the corners of marketplaces anywhere in the world. These old business models, once disappeared through the movement of capitalism to promote rationalization and streamlining, have revived with "new values" at the advent of the Internet revolution. This is a value-added revival because the old methods of "bidding" and "limit price" could only handle several hundred people at most, but "auction" and "reverse auction" over the Internet can deal with millions of people.

Additionally, "e-mail" used by most people now is a revival of "letters" that had faded away behind the spread of the telephone. However, unlike letters of the past, e-mail is a medium by which we can instantly communicate with people on the other side of the Earth and send the same message to tens of thousands of people simultaneously.

Another instance is "e-learning," a widespread method of education nowadays. It is not simply a system of "distance learning" but is precisely a revival of temple schools or private tutor system of the past, or in other words, a revival of "individualized learning" system where learners can coordinate their learning in accordance with their own interests, abilities and convenience.

Furthermore, the emergence of "digital democracy" that resulted from the spread of the Internet is in a sense a revival of the old "direct democracy."

As seen above, in this modern age there are countless instances of the "law of spiral development," that is, revivals of old and nostalgic things with new values.

Things Which Oppose and Compete with Each Other Come to Resemble Each Other

Then, what is the second law?

It is the "law of interpenetration of opposing objects."

This law means that "Things which oppose and compete with each other come to resemble each other."

There are countless specific instances of this as well.

For instance, in the beginning of the Internet revolution, the phrase "Net versus Real" was often used, but what occurred in reality was the interpenetration of "Net" and "Real." At present, there is no Real business without utilizing the Net, nor Net business without considering using Real operations such as inventory control and product shipments.

For another instance, "banks" and "stockbrokerage firms," which have the opposing operational focuses of "indirect financing" versus "direct financing," are starting to incorporate the finance operations of each other in the course of relaxation of regulations, thus mutually evolving into "universal banks."

Furthermore, interpenetration often occurs in policies of different political parties as well, through parties' competition to win over each other in reflecting the needs of the electorate. The policies of two opposing parties come to resemble each other as they incorporate the good parts of the policies of their opponents. For instance, the policies of the Conservative Party and the Labor Party in the United Kingdom resemble each other. The policies of Tony Blair's Labor Party were very similar to those of Margaret Thatcher's Conservative Party.

And then, when we look back at our human history, we see that the interpenetration between "capitalism" and "socialism" has occurred as well. There is the one-sided view that capitalism won the battle over socialism, but what happened in reality was the interpenetration of the two. That is, from a historical viewpoint, capitalism has adopted socialism's welfare and other policies while socialism has adopted the market principles of capitalism, which is precisely the occurrence of interpenetration. However, capitalism has successfully evolved through quick adoption of socialism's welfare policies, whereas socialism has failed to adopt capitalism's market principles with the same ease. This is the reason that many of the socialist nations suffered setbacks. On the other hand, such nations as Russia, China and Vietnam, where socialist systems have been dominant, are now realizing economic growth by adopting the principles of capitalism.

This is the "law of interpenetration of opposing objects."

The Pendulum Always Swings to

the Opposite Direction at the End Point

Then, what is the third law?

It is the "law of development through negation of negation."

This law means that "The pendulum always swings to the opposing direction at the end point."

This means that a movement in the world occurs in negation of something, but when the movement reaches the end point, then that movement of negation is negated, triggering a new movement toward the reverse direction.

This movement very much resembles a swinging pendulum that moves toward one direction and reverses its direction at the end point.

There are so many specific instances of this as well.

One of them is the countless number of the "Internet stockbrokerage firms" that were founded as a result of the Internet revolution. Those Net brokerage firms strictly focused on "brokerage services" of stocks without involving "information services" that the conventional stockbrokerage firms had provided, thus creating intense "price competition" and then achieving rapid growth. However, a reversal occurred at the end point of this price competition.

That is, as the price competition intensified, it reached the point where the price of "brokerage services" could not be lowered any further, so those Net brokerage firms also decided to turn their direction toward offering high value-added "information services." This is an instance of pendulum reversal.

Another instance is the evolution of convenience stores in Japan. This business model, in contrast with individual local stores which were once seen in any town and in any region, provided nationwide-uniform products and services through introducing information systems and operating manuals. However, now that the nationwide uniformity has become the norm as a consequence of severe competition within the convenience store industry, a reversal is starting to take place.

That is, some of the companies in the convenience store industry started to employ the strategy of "individualism," where they focus on leveraging the traditions, cultures, characteristics and uniqueness of each region to realize customized store designs and operations as well as a unique product lineup. In other words, once-negated "locally-based individualism" has revived as a "new form of individualism," just like a pendulum reversing its direction at the end point.

Furthermore, with regard to policies of nations, their pendulums will reverse their direction as well in the long term. The pendulums in such issues as "big government versus small government," "government regulations versus free competition," and "relief for the weak versus self-help" are swinging back and forth in-between the two end points according to the situations of the times.

This is the "law of development through negation of negation."

In addition, there are two other laws in dialectic.

The fourth law is the "law of development through transformation from quantity to quality."
The fifth law is the "law of development through sublation of contradiction."

Readers who would like to learn more about these laws including the two above may refer to the book mentioned earlier.

As stated previously, the most effective laws of the five in foreseeing the future of capitalism are the "three laws" that have just been discussed.

If we base these "three laws" in foreseeing the evolution of capitalism, the paradigm shifts in economic principles underlying capitalism, and future events in capitalist societies, it is possible to see various future scenarios.

Now let us continue our discussions with these "three laws" of dialectic in mind.

In economic principles underlying capitalism, what kinds of changes will happen from now?

Finally, let us enter into this subject.

Chapter 3

The Paradigm Shift
from "Operationalism Economy"
to "Complexity Economy"

How Should We Cope with

"Butterfly Economy"?

What is the first paradigm shift that is beginning to occur in economic principles?

The paradigm shift from "operationalism economy" to "complexity economy."

This is what is occurring.

Now, what is "operationalism economy"?
And what is "complexity economy"?

To facilitate understanding, let us explore "complexity economy" first.
"Complexity economy" refers to the state of economies where the systems of companies, markets and societies have become extremely sophisticated "complex systems."

Then, what are "complex systems"?
The concept of "complex systems" underwent a worldwide

boom in the mid 1990s. Triggered by writings including Mitchell Waldrop's *Complexity: The Emerging Science at the Edge of Order and Chaos*, the worldwide boom took place and many related publications were read. In the midst of this boom, the Santa Fe Institute in New Mexico, the United States, moved into the international spotlight.

As is widely known, the institute was founded in 1984 by three Nobel Prize-winning scholars, Murray Gell-Mann and Philip Anderson in Physics and Kenneth Arrow in Economic Science. The institute hosts a number of high-spirited researchers from various disciplines—physics, chemistry, biology, psychology, cultural anthropology, history, sociology, politics, economics, computer science and others—to literally realize an interdisciplinary approach to the study of "complex systems." In other words, "complex systems" is a highly extensive interdisciplinary subject at the leading edge of modern science.

Although many people must have read about "complex systems" in the midst of the boom, there must be a lot of people who actually feel: "I don't quite understand what complex systems are."

I am involved in the study of "complex systems" as a faculty member of the New England Complex Systems Institute (NECSI) in Boston, the United States and have authored a couple of books that explain "complex systems" in an easily comprehensible manner: *Management of Complex Systems* and *Knowledge of Complex Systems* (both available in Japanese; yet to be published in English). Below, I will state the essential points on "complex systems."

What are "complex systems"?
To state simply, they are "living systems."
This fact is symbolized in the following words once mentioned by the cultural anthropologist Gregory Bateson:

"In complex things, life dwells."

Just as in his insight, any systems that have increased in complexity, including those of physics, chemistry, biology, psychology, culture, society, politics, and economics, begin to behave as if they were living creatures.

Although study is in progress to analyze this property of complex systems through the approach of "complexity science" by leading edge institutes worldwide, including the Santa Fe Institute, I cannot help but feel impressed by the fact that this insight of Bateson's was presented far in advance of the birth of complexity science.

Then, what does it mean to "behave as if they were living creatures"?

The meaning of this is often represented with the following terms in the study of complex systems:

Self-organization, emergence, the formation of ecosystem, co-evolution, the butterfly effect.

"Self-organization" is a process whereby order, structure and organization are naturally formed in the absence of artificial outside forces. "Emergence" is a process whereby order, structure and organization are naturally born while each component ("agent") within the system behaves freely. The "formation of ecosystem" is a process whereby one orderly system is formed through the organic connection of each agent. "Co-evolution" is a process whereby each of the different systems undergoes evolution while affecting each other. And the "butterfly effect" is a phenomenon where a slight fluctuation within a system causes an enormous change in the entire system.

These phenomena are just like "behaviors of living creatures" and should be referred to as "living system phenomena."

However, what complexity science attempts to reveal is not simply the mechanisms of "phenomena that resemble the behaviors of living creatures." Actually, what this science is seeking is the answer to this fundamental question: "What is living system?" The definition of what life is will undergo dramatic changes in the near future as complexity science advances.

Why Are Economies Becoming "Complex Systems"?

Now, let us return to the topic of "economies."

Since "complex systems" are "living systems," "complexity economy" is precisely the state of "economies where the properties of living systems are dominant."

Then, what is the problem with "complexity economy"?

It is the "butterfly effect."

The largest problem that arises as economic systems significantly acquire the properties of "complex systems" is the "butterfly effect" described earlier.

When a system increases in complexity, a slight fluctuation in the corner of the system causes an enormous change in the entire system. Therefore, when "societies" as systems increase in complexity, a slight fluctuation in the corner of a society causes an enormous change in the entire society. Likewise, when "economies" as systems increase in complexity, a slight fluctuation in the corner of a market causes an enormous change in the entire market.

The subprime mortgage crisis ("subprime crisis" hereafter) would be a typical instance of this effect. The collapse of housing loans in the United States triggered the global economic crisis and global recession. This is precisely the butterfly effect.

Of course, the butterfly effect does not always occur as a "negative effect"; it often occurs as a "positive effect."

For instance, there is the case of Google, where a company that started as a small venture eventually caused a fundamental change in the way the entire world shares information as well as a dramatic change in the way businesses function.

However, when considering "complexity economy," we should deeply consider the risk that a "negative effect" can occur all at once involving the entire world.

The subprime crisis teaches us that.

Then, in the first place, why does the butterfly effect occur in complex systems?

This may be slightly difficult, but let us explore it below.

The reason is that the increased complexity in systems causes tighter interrelationships between each agent within the systems, thereby forming "loops" within the systems. The changes that occur within the systems are amplified and accelerated through those loops, resulting in the natural formation of order and structure or, under certain circumstances, in dramatic changes called the butterfly effect.

To present an easily comprehensible instance of the order and structure formation in the world of economy, the formation of a "de facto standard" in markets would be most relevant.

In the past VCR market, for instance, there had been a couple of competing technical standards: the VHS standard and the Betamax standard. However, since VHS was slightly superior to Betamax in recording duration time, film production companies released slightly more films in the VHS format. The number of consumers who preferred VHS over Betamax thus became slightly more. Capturing this trend, film companies began to release even more VHS films, which then led even more consumers to prefer VHS over Betamax. This caused new potential VCR consumers who witnessed the trend to choose VHS as well. As a consequence of this positive loop, the competitive advantage of the VHS standard was reinforced and accelerated, and the VHS standard eventually gained the position as the de facto standard in the VCR market, thus becoming the winner in the market. It is not that VHS was designated to be the standard by an outside force such as governments. The order and structure were born naturally within the market through the processes of self-organization and emergence.

As seen above, in markets as complex systems, various loops are formed, within which the processes of "positive loops" and "negative loops" are generated and then changes are reinforced and accelerated. As a result of this, at times, the processes of self-organization and emergence are promoted, and thus order and structure are naturally created. When the processes of "positive loops" and "negative loops" are intensely accelerated, the dramatic phenomenon called the "butterfly effect" can occur.

Then, why is "complexity economy" a major issue now?

In fact, economies have always possessed the properties of "complex systems."

What symbolizes this fact is the thought of the "invisible hand of God" by Adam Smith: Producers and consumers in a market merely acting freely will naturally lead to the formation of order within the market as if led by the "invisible hand of God." This is precisely the thought of self-organization and emergence and indicates that markets and economies have always possessed the properties of "complex systems."

Then, why should we discuss "complexity economy" now?

The reason for this is clear.

It is because economies have been drastically acquiring the properties of "complex systems" in recent years.

As a consequence, now bubble economies can easily heat up and the butterfly effect, such as the subprime crisis, can easily occur.

Then, why have economies been acquiring the properties of "complex systems" so drastically?

There are three factors for this.

The first factor is the "information revolution."

As a result of the Internet revolution that took place in the mid 1990s, the information networks within societies and markets rapidly expanded, and the interrelationships between companies, organizations, consumers and individuals dramatically increased. Consequently, the complexity of societies and markets drastically increased. This fact is obvious when we count the number of e-mails we handle each day. Before the Internet revolution, the number of people we contacted each day or shared information with was by far lower than that of now.

The second factor is "relaxation of regulation."

The continued "relaxation of regulation" in markets has enabled new players to penetrate into existing markets. In addition, it has also enabled companies of different industries to partner or compete freely beyond the conventional boundary of each industry. Moreover, the increase of outsourcing has led companies to gain more connections with various companies outside their own industry. Due to these conditions, the connections between companies and between organizations in markets have become extremely complex.

The third factor is "globalization."

With the termination of the Cold War between the East and the West, the world has become connected as a single economic bloc. The economy called "global economy" has thus emerged, where the economy and the markets of each nation are closely connected with those of the other side of the Earth affecting each other instantly. Due to such a global network, economies have become even more complex.

In other words, these three factors strengthened the interrelationships within economic systems, increasing the systems' complexity and thereby making already complex economic systems even more complex. This is the primary reason that "complexity economy" is an issue now.

What Is the Largest Problem with "Complexity Economy"?

Now, what is the largest problem with "complexity economy"? The answer to this question is also clear.

"Complexity economy" cannot be manipulated intentionally.

This is the most serious problem.

Complexity economy is the state of economies where the nature of "living systems" is dominant, as represented in processes such as self-organization, emergence, the formation of ecosystem, co-evolution, and the butterfly effect. As such, it cannot be artificially manipulated, managed, controlled, nor led.

These properties of complex systems are very similar to the nature of "living creatures" that cannot be controlled freely. While it is possible to freely manipulate "mechanical systems," it is fundamentally impossible to intentionally manipulate "living systems" that behave as if they had their own minds.

Certainly economic systems have always possessed the nature of "living systems," as described earlier. This fact is represented in long-used terms such as "vitality of economy" and "will of market" as well as in the metaphors "bullish" and "bearish" stock markets.

On the other hand, the attempt has been made in conventional economics to treat the "living systems" of economies as if they were "mechanical systems."

This is symbolized by the application of "mathematical economics" where economic systems are analyzed through mathematical and statistical methods and represented in the form of mathematical models. It is also symbolized by the application of "financial engineering" where the financial market is modeled through mathematical methods and, based on those models, financial products such as derivatives are developed to intentionally maximize profits. The term "financial engineering," as symbolized in the word "engineering" contained in it, strongly reflects people's desire to treat "living systems" of economies and markets as "mechanical systems."

However, the attempt in economics and financial engineering to treat the "living systems" of economies as "mechanical systems" has caused those "living systems" to intensely rebel and avenge. This is the meaning of the current subprime crisis.

Now that "complex systems" have been explained, readers will comprehend the meaning of this other term:

"Operationalism economy."

After all, when looking back, we find that conventional economies have been what should be referred to as "operationalism economy."

The underlying notion of operationalism economy is that we can lead economies and markets to intended directions if we only analyze the "mechanism of economic systems" or the "mechanism of market systems" and then implement government policies or corporate strategies by applying the knowledge on those mechanisms. This notion is symbolized in the terms "policy steering" and "market manipulation" that are used in policymaking. Furthermore, the delusion has emerged that we can intentionally manipulate economies and markets by utilizing the acquired knowledge. This is symbolized by the application of "financial engineering" that involves high-level mathematical methods and also by such financial products as derivatives that were created through financial engineering. However, the notion that "Economies and markets can be manipulated through the knowledge on the economic and market mechanisms" has reached its limit, as described earlier.

What is happening here?

This means that the notion of operationalism has reached its limit. The notion where we consider economies and markets, which are essentially "living systems," to be "mechanical systems" and where we believe we can freely manipulate those systems by analyzing their mechanisms and by utilizing "engineering methods," has reached a point where it is no longer applicable.

As a matter of fact, this "mechanical system worldview" and the "methods of operationalism" that derive from this worldview are the "woes of the times" that hinder the resolution of many problems confronting human society in this 21st century, including not only the current global economic crisis but also the global environmental problems and widespread terrorism. I wish to discuss this subject in detail in another occasion.

As seen above, the economic principles underlying capitalism are now entering into the paradigm shift from "operationalism economy" to "complexity economy."

However, conventional economics unfortunately has not yet established methods for coping with this new "complexity economy," that is, methods for coping with the various living processes that occur in economies and markets as living systems: self-organization, emergence, the formation of ecosystem, co-evolution and the butterfly effect.

One of the largest problems is that no effective methods have been presented within the realm of conventional economics for coping with the butterfly effect, such as the current subprime crisis and the subsequent global economic crisis. In other words, conventional economics has not yet identified methods for coping with "butterfly economy," an economy where the butterfly effect is generated.

How Should We Cope with "Complexity Economy"?

Now, how should we cope with this problem?

Of course, no easy solution to this problem exists, but there are a few important suggestions from the viewpoint of complexity science. Here are the three suggestions for coping with and managing complex systems:

The first suggestion: Complex systems cannot be intentionally designed, built nor managed.

The second suggestion: Complex systems can suddenly break down.

The third suggestion: In complex systems, the emergence process is generated through the behavior of each agent within the systems.

What do these mean? Let us discuss them in the context of economic systems.

The meaning of the first suggestion, "Complex systems cannot be intentionally managed," has been explained in the section where the "limit of operationalism" was discussed. Unlike mechanical systems, complex systems cannot be designed, built nor managed intentionally due to their properties as living systems. Likewise, economies and markets as complex systems cannot be designed, built nor managed either. Due to the properties of economies and markets as living systems, the basic approach for coping with them should be to promote their self-organization and emergence, to foster the formation of an economic ecosystem, and to develop co-evolution within the ecosystem. If we attempt to intentionally design, build and manage the living systems of economies and markets, we will inevitably impair their life force. In fact, this is an issue that has always been raised within the field of economics in the form of "government regulation" versus "free competition" debate. Complexity science indicates that "free competition" should be fully encouraged in order to maximize the life force of economies and markets as living systems. However, this issue cannot be coped with in such a simple manner.

That is because of the existence of the second suggestion by complexity science.

What does "Complex systems can suddenly break down" mean?

Complex systems surely experience evolution through self-organization and emergence processes. However, there is also a possibility that they suddenly break down under certain circumstances. This is what the second suggestion means. In other words, when economies and markets are left to their own devices under the notion that free competition is crucial for generating self-organization and emergence processes, phenomena such as the butterfly effect can occur at times, leading to a sudden breakdown of entire systems.

This is actually very profound; this property of complexity economy provides a warning against a thought that has always been discussed in the realm of conventional economics.

That is, the words "invisible hand of God" by Adam Smith. These words represent the thought that free competition in markets will naturally bring balance and order as if led by the "invisible hand of God." However, in markets as complex systems, while those self-organization and emergence can occur, there is also a possibility that entire systems can break down under certain circumstances. This is what complexity science teaches us. In other words, complexity science teaches us that the "invisible hand of God" does not always lead markets to balance and order; it can at times lead them to catastrophic events, thereby causing the breakdown of the economic systems. We realize this fact through our past experiences with the bursting of economic bubbles, economic crises and other events, and therefore the importance of "government regulation" has been emphasized in the realm of conventional economics as a measure for preventing those catastrophic scenarios.

In this context, it may seem that complexity science highlights the importance of both "free competition" and "government regulation" in economic systems. However, complexity science in fact indicates another extremely important matter. That is the third suggestion:

"In complex systems, the emergence process is generated through the behavior of each agent within the systems."
What does this mean?

It means that the behavior of entire complex systems are determined not by the rules that govern the entire systems but by the behavioral rules of each agent within the systems. That is, in complex systems, a slight shift in the behavioral rules of each agent can lead to completely different emergence or self-organization processes, which in some situations unfortunately leads to the breakdown of the entire systems. In other words, in a complexity economy, a slight shift in the rules of behavior, ethical norms or codes of conduct in companies or individuals within markets can greatly change the consequences of emergence and self-organization processes in the economies and the markets.

As seen above, these "three suggestions" by complexity science provide us with important wisdom for coping with complexity economy. The most important of the three must be the "third suggestion."

The reason is that many of the discussions on the current global economic crisis have fallen into the argument between the two dichotomic notions of "tightening government regulation" and "preserving free competition."

This dichotomic view is reflected in most of the discussions between experts seen in newspapers, magazines and TV programs.

However, here is one fact we should realize:

The methods for coping with complexity economy are not limited to the choice between the two alternatives of "control" and "noninterference."

We need to realize this fact.

What complexity science teaches us is the importance of the "third way."

What is this "third way"?

It is "autonomy."

When we consider the economic order in the post-economic crisis world, we should emphasize the third method the "promotion of self-discipline" in addition to "preserving free competition" and "tightening government regulation." For this purpose, we must first promote the measures for establishing ethical norms and codes of conduct in companies and in individuals from a long-term viewpoint.

The Distortion of "CSR" by Global Capitalism

When the topic "ethical norms and codes of conduct in companies and individuals" is raised, many readers may think of one keyword prevalent in the present time:

"CSR."

This is the keyword. It represents "Corporate Social Responsibility."

As is widely recognized, CSR is a worldwide trend that stems from the incidents involving Enron and WorldCom in 2001 and 2002, and it is a movement whereby companies are demanded to be socially responsible, not just pursue profits for shareholders. The movement has widely spread to the extent where international standards for CSR have recently been established by the International Organization for Standardization (ISO). In advanced capitalist nations, many companies are currently working to practice CSR as they establish ethical norms and codes of conduct as well as requesting their employees to think and act while being aware of their social responsibility.

As mentioned earlier, in order to cope with complexity economy, it is important to factor in not only the methods of "control" and "noninterference" but also "autonomy," and for that purpose to "promote self-discipline" by establishing ethical norms and codes of conduct in companies and individuals. This, in other words, means that the current worldwide trend of "CSR" needs to be considered even more deeply and be practiced in even larger scale in order to cope with complexity economy.

In response to this view, some readers may say: "That is only natural."

That is because the cause of the current subprime crisis and the global economic crisis is that financial companies focusing only on profits have deviated from corporate ethics. People therefore started to voice that "Companies should put a high value on compliance and corporate ethics and be aware of their social responsibility." This is certainly the case.

However, the issue is not that simple.

Because, regarding the meaning of CSR, a great misinterpretation has arisen today.

The various recent scandals and crimes involving companies throughout the world were caused by those companies' intense focus on profit-maximizing activities in the course of the rising "global capitalism," or "market fundamentalism." And what has emerged from reflecting on this experience is the worldwide trend of CSR. Nevertheless, there unfortunately has been a tendency for the CSR trend itself to become distorted due to prevalent arguments regarding the principles of market and of competition proclaimed by global capitalism.

In other words, a distorted interpretation has arisen regarding the concept of CSR.

What kind of interpretation is this?

It is reflected in the following arguments that are now abundant throughout the world:

"Not emphasizing CSR will lead to defeat in the competitive market."

"Not emphasizing CSR will lead to the loss of shareholders' support."

The logic of these arguments seems rational at first. However, there is a major hole in it.

Because, behind this logic are hidden these opposite statements:

"If we can survive in the competitive market, practicing CSR is needless."

"Unless shareholders require us to do so, practicing CSR is needless."

Those arguments are easily replaced with these opposite statements.
What kind of mistake is this?

Positioning CSR in the context of market principles, despite the fact that CSR is essentially a concept beyond the frame of market principles.

This is the mistake.
Additionally, the following arguments are also prevalent:

"Emphasizing CSR will attract talented people to our company and therefore lead to the company's long-term profit."
"Emphasizing CSR will heighten our company's reputation and therefore lead to the company's long-term profit."

Then what kind of mistake is this?

Positioning CSR in the context of profit pursuit, despite the fact that CSR is essentially a concept beyond the dimension of profit pursuit.

This is the mistake.
As mentioned above, these arguments on CSR are abundant in the world. This is symbolically reflected in the book *Creative Capitalism: A Conversation with Bill Gates, Warren Buffet, and Other Economic Leaders* authored by Michael Kinsley. In this book, a number of renowned economists as well as business scholars debate against each other on the concept of "creative capitalism" that is advocated by Bill Gates. In those debates, the four arguments on CSR mentioned above are frequently raised.

"Ethics" Is a Notion beyond Market Principles

Now, why should those arguments be considered misinterpretation?

The reason for this is clear.

Because the notion of "ethics" is essentially beyond the dimension of "competition" or "profits."

To illustrate this more clearly, let us imagine a person.

When asked "Why do you embrace ethics?" this person answers, "Because I cannot be the winner otherwise." How will the people surrounding him view him?

Or his answer may be "Because I can gain profits if I am ethical." How will the people surrounding him view him?

Will they think that he is a "wonderful person"?

As illustrated here, the irrationality of those arguments' logic on corporate ethics can be revealed when it is placed in the context of human ethics. If a company presents the logic illustrated above, will the surrounding consumers think that it is a "wonderful company"?

The answer must be, no.

What we should clearly realize at this point is that "ethics for companies" and "ethics for individuals" essentially must be considered based on the same logic.

Why is this?

Because the ethics of companies, although called "corporate ethics," is to be ultimately practiced by "individuals."

Although it is called "corporate ethics," it is observed not by a notional personality of "juridical persons." It is observed by the "individuals" or the "living persons" who belong to the company organization.

And the "individuals" of greatest responsibility are of course the "president," "CEO" or the "members of top management."

In other words, the "ethical sense" of a company's top management will ultimately determine the company's "sense of ethics."

This fact should never be neglected.

Therefore, when CSR of a company is discussed, ultimately what kind of thoughts the corporate executives have will be a major issue.

This is because the executives who place emphasis on "social responsibility" for the reason that they "cannot be the winner otherwise" will, due to their thoughts, inevitably lose sight of the essential meaning of social responsibility. They will someday start neglecting "social responsibility" for the reason that their companies "cannot be the winner."

Then why should a company, and an executive, place emphasis on social responsibility?

This is because they hold "principles" as a company or as an executive.

A corporate executive who holds firm "principles" as an individual will not lose himself.

A company that holds firm "principles" as an organization will not lose itself.

These "principles" may be called "ideal." It may also be called "aesthetic."

Executives and companies with these "internal norms" will not lose themselves.

Their steadfast operations are not forced by "external norms" such as "punishments" or "profits." Executives and companies that live by the "internal norms" established on their own have a quality that prevents them from being lost.

Therefore, when we consider the way future capitalism should take, the most important method for preserving the order of markets is not "noninterference" nor "control," but it is the third method, "autonomy."

However, in response to the view above, some readers may present the following doubt:

"Executives are humans after all, so they are susceptible to their weakness. They may act wrong as a result. This is precisely why we should tighten regulations and punishments so as to prevent them from doing wrong."

This, in a sense, is a way of policies based on "the view of human nature as inherently evil."

For certain, we must admit that there are unfortunately numerous situations in current society where we need to take this view of human nature. Therefore, adopting policies from this viewpoint may be necessary in reality.

However, there is one matter that we should deeply consider in adopting those policies.

It is the following paradox regarding "view of humans" and "institutions":

Institutions that are formed based on a certain view of humans, as they take root in society, in return increase the number of people to whom those institutions apply.

We should consider this dreadful paradox.

In addition, there is another paradox we should realize:

The society where order is maintained only through regulations and punishments will inevitably bear hidden depravity.

This is the paradox.

In the first place, just tightening control on crimes in a high-crime society will never eradicate crimes. What will truly lead to a decline in crime in the long term is to teach morality and ethics through education and thereby heightening the awareness of individuals. To nurture "autonomous individuals" who choose not to commit crimes is what will lead to a decline in crime.

This must have been a lesson we humans had gained from experiences in our long history.

Therefore, in order to ingrain the spirit of CSR in many companies in our current capitalism, we should place more emphasis on the method of "autonomy" or "promotion of self-discipline."

In other words, an executive should first be demanded as a human being to be moral, ethical and socially responsible without being affected by materialistic views as in "We cannot survive without placing emphasize on CSR" or "Practicing CSR will lead us to profits."

This is neither youthful idealism nor an unrealistic mindset.

This is the way that executives in the past behaved, at least in Japan. This will be discussed in detail later in this book.

Why Will the Companies Practicing CSR Attract "Invisible Capital"?

I will state this again.

CSR is not an activity that we unwillingly emphasize owing to the necessity for survival in market competition.

It is not an activity that we obligatorily practice for avoiding long-term loss of profit, either.

But it is essentially an activity practiced only as "companies' independent and voluntary choice" to comply with laws, to embrace corporate ethics and to fulfill social responsibility.

However, in response to this view, some readers may once again oppose in this manner:

"That spirit is certainly respectable. However, with such an idealistic view, businesses will lose competitiveness and will experience reduced ability to earn profits."

These tempting words that are whispered to many executives today. These irresistible words.

However, the evolution of capitalism in the coming age will actually make those words stale and obsolete.

Because, in the new capitalism emerging now, companies that practice CSR as their independent and voluntary choice will naturally attract the trust of many consumers and empathy from them and attract "invisible capital". The age has begun when this kind of companies will flourish in the market.

Why is this?

It is because another paradigm shift is beginning to occur in economies.

Then, what does this paradigm shift mean?
What does "invisible capital" mean?

Chapter 4

The Paradigm Shift
from "Knowledge Economy"
to "Empathy Economy"

How Should We Evaluate
"Invisible Economy"?

That is the second paradigm shift.

The paradigm shift from "knowledge economy" to "empathy economy."

Now, what is "empathy economy"?

In order to comprehend this, we need to first understand what "knowledge economy" is.

However, in response to the statement above, many readers may feel that "The idea of knowledge economy is all so familiar now" or "I understand it already."

This is because the ideas of "knowledge society," "knowledge economy" and "knowledge capitalism" have been more than fully explained in these past several decades by such experts as Daniel Bell, Alvin Toffler and Peter Drucker; those ideas refer to societies and economies where knowledge and wisdom are the primary resources and capital.

However, I have an opinion from another viewpoint.

It is true that those ideas have been discussed for a long time.

But are the ideas of "knowledge economy" and "knowledge capitalism" incorporated in specific government policies or company strategies?

The answer must be, no.

To state frankly, the reality is that many governments and companies have not fully figured out policies and strategies to cope with knowledge economy and knowledge capitalism.

For instance, let us imagine how corporate executives may respond to this question: "What are your company's strategies for coping with knowledge economy?"

Probably many of them can only mention their limited strategies as in "Our company has established the Intellectual Property Management Office" or "Our company strives to protect patents and intellectual property rights."

Additionally, let us imagine how administrative officials may respond to this question: "What are your policies with regard to knowledge capitalism?"

Probably many of them can only say: "We are working to enhance research functions in universities and institutes" or "We are working to nurture creative human resources in our nation."

Their limited answers can be attributed to their inadequate understanding of knowledge economy and knowledge capitalism; they see that the value of knowledge economy is in "patents" and "intellectual properties" and consider knowledge capitalism to be the notion under which they compete on developing "research and development capacity" and "creative human resources."

Then why is this "inadequate understanding"?

It is due to the fact that as knowledge economy deepens, "knowledge capital" is expanding in its definition to cover broader concepts. That is, the definition of "knowledge capital" is now not limited to the dimension of "patents" and "intellectual properties" and the sources of those values such as "excellent human resources" and "brainpower"; it is expanding to also cover higher-level concepts of capital, such as "relation capital," "trust capital," "brand capital" and "culture capital."

The largest problem in economics in the age of knowledge economy and knowledge capitalism is that no specific methods have been created for evaluating and handling "knowledge capital," "relation capital," "trust capital," "brand capital" and "culture capital."

Let us discuss the meaning of these different types of capital in detail later.

Why Cannot Conventional Economics Handle "Knowledge Capital"?

Why is it difficult in conventional economics to evaluate and handle "knowledge capital," "relation capital," "trust capital," "brand capital" and "culture capital"?

It is because the types of capital that have been handled in conventional economics are only those that can be evaluated by the objective measure of currency, that is, "visible capital," while "knowledge capital," "relation capital," "trust capital," "brand capital" and "culture capital" are "invisible capital," the types of capital that cannot be evaluated by the measure of currency.

Nevertheless, conventional economics has attempted to forcefully convert "invisible capital" into "visible capital" when conducting the evaluation. For instance, the value of patents and intellectual properties has been converted into monetary value to be entered on financial statements. In this way, "knowledge capital" has been evaluated through its conversion into "monetary capital."

What has been done here?

This means that the new economic paradigm called "knowledge economy" has been evaluated with the economic scale of the old economic paradigm called "monetary economy."

Then, what does the word "invisible" contained in the term "invisible capital" mean?

It does not simply mean "cannot be evaluated by the visible measure of currency"; it is actually more profound.

This is because "knowledge capital," aside from being immeasurable with currency, possesses three characteristics that are extremely difficult to handle.

It would be extremely important to understand these characteristics in order to comprehend the essence of knowledge economy and knowledge capitalism.

What are those three characteristics?

They are the following:

"It cannot be owned."
"It grows by itself."
"It transforms."

What do these mean?

For instance, a company may acquire another company that employs a number of excellent engineers who own many patents and conduct various inventive projects, but there is a possibility that these knowledgeable and wise human resources may leave the company.

This is what "It cannot be owned" means.

Additionally, a group of people without any excellent ideas or plans at first may later develop new ideas or plans by sharing knowledge and wisdom within the group.

This is what "It grows by itself" means.

Moreover, a person who does not have a certain knowledge or wisdom himself may "borrow wisdom" by building relations with those who do. Thus, a person's lack of certain knowledge and wisdom can be covered by the relations with those who have the knowledge and wisdom. In other words, "knowledge and wisdom" transform into an indirect form called "relations."

This is what "It transforms" means.

These three characteristics are the reasons that we cannot enter "knowledge capital" on financial statements in a visible quantitative form and therefore we cannot evaluate and handle it within the realm of conventional economics.

Knowledge Capital Transforms into "Meta-level" Forms

Of these three characteristics, the third one is especially important.

The reason for this is that knowledge capital often changes its form to develop into "broadly-defined capital," or "meta-level capital" in other words, as illustrated below:

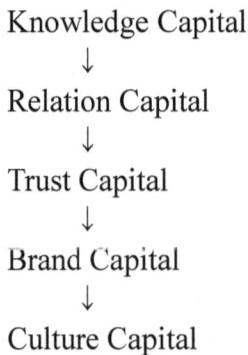

Knowledge Capital
↓
Relation Capital
↓
Trust Capital
↓
Brand Capital
↓
Culture Capital

What does this mean?

As mentioned earlier, the knowledge we lack ourselves can be easily borrowed through good relations with knowledgeable companies or people. Therefore, having good relations with many companies and people, that is, having abundant capital called "relations," is in a sense equivalent to indirectly having abundant "knowledge capital." In other words, "relation capital" is "broadly-defined knowledge capital" or "meta-level knowledge capital."

Additionally, even in the absence of good "relations" with knowledgeable companies or people, having social "trust" can facilitate good relation building. For instance, our networks of contacts are often extended through "referrals by trusted acquaintances." It would be difficult to start good relations with people who might suddenly contact us by phone without a previous referral and say: "I would like to work with you." Thus, having "trust" with people is equivalent to having abundant "trust capital," which in a sense means indirectly having abundant "relation capital." In other words, "trust capital" is "broadly-defined relation capital" or "meta-level relation capital."

Moreover, even in the absence of direct trusted relations, having high social "recognition" or a good public "reputation" may facilitate "trust." For instance, when meeting an intellect for the first time, we may say: "I have heard so much about your accomplishments." This is a situation where trust is naturally formed due to the information about the intellect's high social reputation. It is also possible to gain trust just by holding a title in a company with a strong brand image. Thus, having a good public "reputation" is equivalent to having abundant "brand capital," which in a sense means indirectly having abundant "trust capital." In other words, "brand capital" is "broadly-defined trust capital" or "meta-level trust capital."

"High social recognition" and a "good public reputation" as described above are not of the nature that can be formed through self-promotion or company PR strategies. They ultimately come from "humanity" in the case of a person and from the "corporate culture" for a company. Conversely, companies with "excellent culture" will definitely establish "high reputation in the society" and "deep trust from customers" as well as "good relations with other companies." Thus, having excellent "corporate culture" is equivalent to having abundant "culture capital," which in a sense means indirectly having abundant "brand capital," "trust capital," "relation capital" and "knowledge capital." In other words, "culture capital" is broadly-defined or meta-level "brand capital," "trust capital," "relation capital" and "knowledge capital."

As illustrated above, in the coming age of knowledge economy and knowledge capitalism, while "narrowly-defined knowledge capital" such as patents and intellectual properties will be of importance, "broadly-defined knowledge capital" or "meta-level knowledge capital" will be even more important. This latter kind of capital includes "knowledge capital" such as knowledge and wisdom of employees and customers, "relation capital" such as relations with customers and other companies, "trust capital" and "brand capital" such as trust and reputation in the society, and "culture capital" such as organizational culture within companies.

However, in response to this view, some readers may present the following opinion:

"The ideas of 'knowledge,' 'relations,' 'trust,' 'reputation' and 'culture' must have always been precious assets in the business world. Why should we be discussing their value further at this point in time?"

This is certainly true.

Needless to use the terms "knowledge economy" or "knowledge capitalism," anyone who has gone through the world of business naturally realizes from his or her experiences that such qualities have always been highly valuable.

Then why should we discuss such kinds of capital as "knowledge capital," "relation capital," "trust capital," "brand capital" and "culture capital" in terms of "knowledge economy" and "knowledge capitalism"?

There are two clear reasons for this.

The first reason is that there is a prevailing tendency for people not to value those types of "invisible capital."

Since "global capitalism" has been dominating the world with commanding influence in recent years, there has been a tendency worldwide for any type of values to be converted into "monetary value" and for any type of capital to be reduced to "monetary capital." Therefore, we need to discuss this "invisible capital" in a way as an antithesis of this world-dominating notion that should be referred to as "monetary reductionism."

The second reason is that as a result of a certain revolution those types of "invisible capital" have become visible and increased in influence.

Needless to say, the revolution is the Internet revolution that began in the mid 1990s.

It enabled anybody to utilize web sites and blogs as well as to join Bulletin Board Systems and the Net communities. As a consequence, qualities such as knowledge, relations, trust, reputation (brand) and culture have become "visible" and began exerting commanding influence in businesses and societies. This tendency has been accelerated even more since the mid 2000s as the Internet revolution advanced to the stage referred to as the Web 2.0 revolution.

Then, what will happen from now as a consequence?

Let us state this simply.

Due to the Internet revolution and the Web 2.0 revolution, the value of "knowledge," "relations," "trust," "reputation (brand)" and "culture" will be overwhelmingly enhanced and therefore these types of "invisible capital" will rapidly gain influence. This will then deepen the paradigm of knowledge economy, leading to the evolution of capitalism itself to an even higher level of knowledge capitalism.

I have discussed the scenario of capitalism evolving through the Internet revolution in one of my books: *What Will Happen From Now On?: The Web 2.0 Revolution Will Change Everything in*

Capitalism; available in Japanese.

As illustrated above, in the future capitalism, "invisible capital" such as knowledge, relations, trust, brand and culture will be extremely important. Therefore, we will need to establish new theories and methods for evaluating these types of "invisible capital" or "meta-level knowledge capital" as well as new strategies and policies to grow these types of capital.

Then what should we call the "meta-level knowledge capital" of knowledge, relations, trust, brand and culture as a whole?

"Empathy capital."

This is what we should call it.
This is because what underlies all of these five types of capital is "empathy."
For instance, where knowledge and wisdom are born, there always exists empathy.
In the brainstorming method, where people share ideas and wisdom, it is often mentioned that the basic rule should be "not to criticize others' ideas." This is because the place where people harshly criticize each other lacks "empathy" and impedes the cultivation of novel ideas and wisdom.
Likewise, where good relations are born, there always exists "empathy" between humans. On the other hand, it is possible that human relations may start only through the "thought of private gain" or "calculation," but we all realize from our past experiences that those types of relations can never develop into "productive relations" nor "creative relations."
Needless to say, "trust," "brand" and "culture" are the qualities that are born through "empathy" between humans, such as the "empathy" from consumers to companies and the "empathy" between co-workers in the workplace.

As seen above, in the future capitalism, "empathy capital" as a whole— "knowledge capital," "relation capital," "trust capital," "brand capital" and "culture capital" —will become extremely important.

Nevertheless, conventional economics has not yet established theories and methods for evaluating "invisible capital," or "meta-level knowledge capital," or "empathy capital" that possesses those unique characteristics.

"Invisible Capital" That Has Been Impaired by the Subprime Crisis

Now, there is one matter we should realize in particular:

As knowledge economy and knowledge capitalism mature, the importance of "trust capital," "brand capital" and "culture capital" will become greater than that of "knowledge capital" and "relation capital."

This is what we should realize.

The reason for this is that while "trust capital," "brand capital" and "culture capital" require time and effort to form, they will, once formed, merge with the type of capital called "social capital" and become the "strongest capital" for the company.

Then, what is "social capital"?

Discussing this subject will require much space, and therefore only the main points will be outlined below.

In past industrial societies, the term "social capital" primarily referred to hard infrastructures in societies such as roads, railways, waterworks and electrical power lines. However, as industrial societies evolve into information societies and next into knowledge societies, the definition of social capital has expanded to include not only hard infrastructures but also soft infrastructures. "Knowledge capital," "relation capital," "trust capital," "brand capital" and "culture capital" have thus become to be considered a part of socially-accumulated capital.

The most symbolic instance of this would be the case of Silicon Valley in the United States.

A question often asked of Silicon Valley is this: "Why are so many venture businesses born in Silicon Valley?"

The answers to this question may vary, but the most succinct answer is probably represented in the following words:

"It is due to the rich 'business ecosystem' that exists in the region."

This means that there is an ecosystem in Silicon Valley in which various businesses are naturally formed.

Nevertheless, when groups of inspectors from companies and local governments in other countries are dispatched to Silicon Valley, the region is often observed only at a superficial level, leaving the essence of this business ecosystem unexplored. These missions are then concluded with reports of the following kinds:

"There are ample incubation facilities in Silicon Valley." (physical capital)

"Stanford University is cultivating young and excellent entrepreneurs." (human capital)

"This region is thoroughly supported by venture capital funding." (financial capital)

However, the strength of Silicon Valley rather lies in "something invisible" that is behind these physical capital, human capital and financial capital. For instance, behind these three types of capital is abundant "invisible capital," which can be described as follows:

In Silicon Valley, there are not only physical incubation facilities but also the rich knowledge and wisdom on incubation that have been accumulated within the region in the form of human resources such as consultants and advisors. (knowledge capital)

Stanford University alumni are building close networks of relations based on rich empathy among excellent human resources who have gathered from around the world. (relation capital)

In Silicon Valley, opinions about and the reputation of an entrepreneur, whether positive or negative, spread quickly. (trust capital and brand capital)

The local culture exists where an unsuccessful entrepreneur may be praised for the important know-how gained through his or her business failure. (culture capital)

As seen above, the strength of Silicon Valley in a sense lies in the strength of "social capital" that has been accumulated within the community, such as "knowledge capital," "relation capital," "trust capital," "brand capital" and "culture capital." This is precisely the essence of the "business ecosystem" of Silicon Valley.

Now the characteristics of "invisible capital" and "meta-level knowledge capital" have been explained. By taking the viewpoint of "meta-level knowledge capital," the essence of the subprime crisis can be clearly revealed.

If so, what is the essence of the subprime crisis?

It was actually an incident where the profit-chasing financial companies pursued the maximization of "financial capital" through making full use of the methods of operationalism so enthusiastically that they completely destroyed "trust capital," "brand capital" and "culture capital" that should be extremely valuable for societies and companies. This is reflected in the fact that nobody can now straightforwardly trust even the "AAA" ratings.

In other words, the subprime crisis is an absurd incident where the financial industry pursued "visible value" so intensely that they completely destroyed "invisible value," a more precious value than "visible value."

This is the essence of the subprime crisis, and in this sense, the crisis should be viewed as an incident where the "immaturity" of the current state of capitalism was symbolized.

What Is "Maturity" of Capitalism?

Then, what is "maturity" of capitalism?

The answer can actually be found in the following question:

What is "maturity" of the human mind?

The answer to this question is clear.

It is to become to see "invisible things."

As the human mind matures, it becomes able to see "invisible things."

Such as "people's feelings."

We are only able to see "ourselves" in our youth.
We therefore are not able to see the "feelings of others."
However, as our minds mature through various experiences and hardships, we begin to perceive the "feelings of others."
When we develop to play a leadership role in a group of people, we gradually become to sense the surrounding situation and the atmosphere, that is, the "feelings of the group."

Furthermore, as the human mind matures, it also becomes able to see "invisible values."

Such as "cultures."

"Cultures" are qualities that cannot be seen in the absence of a mature mind.

For instance, there is the culture of "sincere hospitality" in Japan, a good old tradition.

This hospitality culture can never be seen by those who believe that "services" mean a prescribed set of services.

In other words, "maturity" of the human mind means that it becomes able to see "invisible values."

If so, what is "maturity of corporate management"?

What is "maturity of capitalism," which will be required in the coming age?

It is precisely the birth of corporate management that considers not only "visible value" but also "invisible value."

And it is precisely the birth of capitalism that considers not only "visible capital" but also "invisible capital."

Now, in order to explore the deeper meaning of "invisible capital," we should realize that another paradigm shift is beginning to occur in economic principles.

What is this another paradigm shift?

Chapter 5

The Paradigm Shift

from "Monetary Economy"

to "Voluntary Economy"

How Should We Utilize

"Shadow Economy"?

The paradigm shift from "monetary economy" to "voluntary economy."

This is the third paradigm shift.

To begin with, what is the largest trap that people tend to fall into when discussing modern capitalism?

It is to assume that "monetary economy" is the only type of economy.

Readers who have read up to this point must realize that this assumption is not correct.

Because, as explored in the discussion of the second paradigm shift, there are not only the "visible capital" of "money" but also "invisible capital" such as "knowledge," "relation," "trust," "brand" and "culture," and moreover, economies that are based on these types of invisible capital are now increasing.

However, there is another profound meaning in the statement "Monetary economy is not the only type of economy."

It is the fact that different economic principles had been prevalent before "monetary economy" began.

This is just as discussed in Chapter 1.

When we reflect on the history of humankind, we realize that economic principles have actually evolved through the following "three steps."

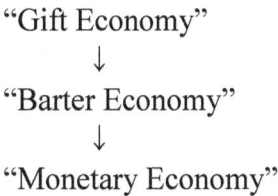

"Gift Economy"
↓
"Barter Economy"
↓
"Monetary Economy"

Before "monetary economy" began and established overwhelming dominance in the world, "barter economy" had been prevalent.

It is the type of economy where valuable goods are directly exchanged between people.

Exchange of goods is still a daily practice between people in societies where monetary economy is underdeveloped; for instance, they may exchange grain for fish. Moreover, even in societies where monetary economy is fully developed, this activity is conducted as "barter trading" at times.

Furthermore, before "barter economy" began, "gift economy" had been a prevalent economic principle.

It is the type of economy where valuable goods are given to others through goodwill and affection.

One instance of this, among others, is a tradition of "potlatch," a ceremonial practice of indigenous people in North America in which they give their valuable goods to each other. Moreover, even in societies where monetary economy is fully developed, the economic principle of "gift economy" has existed in the form of "voluntary economy" and has been a primary economic principle in societies.

Nevertheless, we tend to unconsciously assume when discussing current capitalism that an economic activity only means "monetary economy" which is created for the purpose of "acquisition of money."

However, "voluntary economy," which is an economic activity created by people seeking "satisfaction of mind" based on goodwill and affection, has been playing an extremely important role in our society. We should never forget this fact.

There are countless cases of voluntary economy in our daily life.

For instance, housework, child care, education and elderly care in the home, as well as securing public safety and cleaning activities in communities, are all activities of voluntary economy. None of these activities involve monetary compensation; they are conducted solely based on people's voluntary choice.

In fact, voluntary economy has been an extremely important economic principle that has supported our societies ever since the history of humankind began up to the present.

This fact is obvious when we imagine this one situation:

What would happen if such a thing as "education in the home" disappeared in our society?

Even with the existence of fully-developed public education systems, the missed opportunities to receive discipline and emotional education at a young age would produce a number of individuals who lack cooperativeness and social skills, which would then lead to insufficient workforces in society, resulting in the inability to sustain capitalism itself.

As illustrated above, voluntary economy has been a crucial economic principle that has always supported our societies throughout the long history of humankind up to the present.

The Two Reasons That

Voluntary Economy Has Been Regarded

as a "Shadow Economy"

Nevertheless, voluntary economy has long been placed in the position of a "shadow economy" in the history of humankind.

There are two reasons for this.

The first reason is that voluntary economy was an "invisible economic activity"; it has been invisible to many people since it cannot be evaluated by the objective measure of "currency."

The second reason is that it used to be an "economic activity in the corner of society" that was conducted within homes and communities.

However, voluntary economy, or "shadow economy," is now rapidly increasing in its scale of activities and in impact within society.

Why is this?

It is due to the "Internet revolution."

The Internet revolution that began in the mid 1990s has dramatically increased "voluntary economic activity" in societies.

This is because the revolution has enabled many people to voluntarily set up web sites and blogs as well as to join the Net communities to share various information and knowledge without compensation.

For instance, countless knowledge communities have been born in the Internet world. If we visit online communities called "Q&A

sites," people with specialist knowledge can give us answers to any question without compensation.

Additionally, there are a number of so-called "open source projects," such as the "Linux Project" that is conducted on the Internet by numerous computer engineers who are voluntarily gathering from around the world without compensation to continuously develop and improve the operating system.

Unlike the "conventional voluntary economy" that has long been placed in the position of a "shadow economy," the "new voluntary economy" that resulted from the Internet revolution possesses two features as described below.

The first is that voluntary economy has become an "economic activity that is visible to many people."

Although the voluntary activities in the Internet world cannot be evaluated by the objective measure of "currency," they have become "visible" to anybody since they are publicly shown through web sites and blogs. Additionally, they can be evaluated by objective measures such as "the number of subscribers," "the number of visitors" or "the number of community members."

The second is that voluntary economy has become an "economic activity that bears impact on the entire world."

In the voluntary activities in the Internet world, as symbolized by the "Linux Project," people can put out information to the entire world via web sites and blogs as well as bring together members from all over the world. Thus, voluntary economy is no longer an economic activity "in the corner of society" that is conducted only within homes and communities.

As illustrated above, voluntary economy, which has long been placed in the position of a "shadow economy" despite its having the longest history in human society, is now reviving as a mainstream type of economy as it increases in impact due to the Internet revolution.

The Spiral Development Occurring

in "Economic Principles"

What is happening here?

"Spiral development" is occurring.

As descried in Chapter 2, according to the "law of spiral development" in the Dialectic of Hegel, the world progresses and develops as if it were climbing a spiral staircase.

When looked at from the side of the staircase, it is developing and progressing upward, while it is going around the staircase and returning to the original place when looked at from above. This can be viewed as a revival or restoration of an old and nostalgic thing. Except, as this is a spiral staircase, it is at one level higher each time a circuit is completed.

Thus, in spiral development, old and nostalgic things revive with new values.

From this viewpoint, certainly, "spiral development" is occurring in economic principles as a result of the Internet revolution.

The old and nostalgic voluntary economy is reviving as it increases in impact relative to "monetary economy" that occupies overwhelming mainstream position in current society.

However, it is not like the past voluntary economy that was an "invisible economic activity" or an "economic activity in the corner of society." Through the Internet, it has become an economic activity that is visible to many people and that bears impact on the entire world, thus reviving with new values.

Then, if voluntary economy is reviving through the "law of spiral development" in the Dialectic of Hegel, what will happen next?

The Dialectic of Hegel will occur again.

Another law of dialectic, "interpenetration of opposing objects," will occur.

To state concretely, the development of economic principles will occur based on the "law of development through interpenetration of opposing objects," the law which means that things which are opposing and in competition will merge into one. As a consequence, monetary economy and voluntary economy, which have long been considered to be opposite principles, will begin merging into one from now.

However, in response to these statements above, some readers may present this question: "Isn't it just a theoretical prediction?"
No, it is not.
It has become a reality already.

As a matter of fact, many of the instances of the "development through interpenetration of opposing objects" are also a result of the Internet revolution.
Most easily comprehensible instance is the case of Amazon.com, a bookseller on the Internet.
As is widely known, the company has realized an extremely high-revenue business model which should be considered the best practice business of monetary economy.
Then, what is the most popular service at the Amazon website?
It is the "grassroots review" service.
Those book reviews are read by every customer who considers purchasing a book at the Amazon website.
However, this popular service is not actually provided by the

company. The reviews are written voluntarily by a number of site users and readers without receiving monetary compensation. This means that the service is born through voluntary economy.

As seen above, the business model of Amazon is in fact a model formed through the merging of monetary economy and voluntary economy.

Another instance is the case of Google, a company that was founded in 1998 and has realized rapid growth.

This company has also realized extremely high-revenue business model based on "advertisement services." However, its search engine service is actually provided to users free of charge. Additionally, most of the "mashup" services, which are produced by adding external functions provided by other companies and users to the base functions of Google, are offered voluntarily and free of charge. Thus, the business model of Google is also a model formed through the merging of monetary economy and voluntary economy.

Likewise, the operating system "Linux," born from voluntary economy, has led to the creation of for-profit businesses including "Red Hat" that provide system services around Linux.

As illustrated above, these instances should be referred to as "hybrid economy," the merging of monetary economy and voluntary economy. This means that the dialectic development of economic principles, triggered by the Internet revolution, is now creating this new economic principle.

The Birth of the New Economic Principle

"Hybrid Economy"

Now, is the movement of "hybrid economy" seen only in the Internet world?

No, it is not.

For instance, the worldwide trend of "CSR" that was discussed in Chapter 3.

It is a movement toward "corporate social responsibility," which is spreading primarily in developed capitalist nations as well as in others.

This is a movement where for-profit companies, which have traditionally based their activities on the "pursuit of profits," begin to place emphasis on "social responsibility" and "social contribution" as well. This, in a sense, is a movement where "voluntary economy" is incorporated into "monetary economy."

On the other hand, there is another worldwide trend, the trend of "social entrepreneurship."

This is a movement where non-profit organizations, which have traditionally based their activities on "social contribution," work to generate "profits" from their own operations to ensure their long-term sustainability. This, in a sense, is a movement where "monetary economy" is incorporated into "voluntary economy."

As illustrated above, economic principles that underlie capitalism are now entering into a major paradigm shift. The shift begins with the increased impact of "voluntary economy" relative to the conventional "monetary economy" and then moves to the merging stage of those two economic principles, which will lead to create the new economic principle that should be referred to as "hybrid economy."

That is, what will occur from now is the paradigm shift from "monetary economy" to "voluntary economy," and then to "hybrid economy."

This is the third paradigm shift.

Then, what will further occur in capitalism at that point?

Another fundamental paradigm shift will occur.

Chapter 6

The Paradigm Shift
from "Beneficiary Economy"
to "Participatory Economy"

The "Economy That Unifies Subject and Object" Will Begin

That is the fourth paradigm shift.

The paradigm shift from "beneficiary economy" to "participatory economy" will occur.

Now, what is "beneficiary economy"?
Traditionally, companies have been playing a role as the developers of products and services in markets, while consumers have been in the position to passively "benefit" from those products and services. This is how the conventional market economy has functioned, and this paradigm should be referred to as "beneficiary economy."

However, in the coming age, consumers will not only passively "benefit" from those products and services but also begin to "participate" in the development process of those products and services as they collaborate with or play an alternate role for companies. This is a paradigm that should be referred to as "participatory economy" and will be a major trend in the market economy toward the future. Furthermore, in the coming age, consumers will begin to participate not only in the "development" process of products and services but also in the "design," the "production," the "sales" and the "promotion" processes.

Then, what triggers this paradigm shift?

Again, it is the Internet revolution.

Due to the Internet revolution, "participatory economy" is now rapidly expanding.

An instance that symbolizes the expansion of this type of economy is "prosumer-based development" that has become prevalent in the Internet world in recent years. This is a development method where "companies" (producers) and "customers" (consumers) collaborate in the process of creating new products and services.

This method was predicted by Alvin Toffler three decades ago in his publication *The Third Wave* as he coined the term "pro-sumer." Many consumers now gather in advanced "prosumer communities" in the Internet world where they discuss the needs for various products and services as well as share ideas on new products and services. Additionally, the companies that join in those communities capture the expressed needs and ideas of consumers to incorporate into the development of new products and services as well as to make improvements based on their opinions.

Thus, "prosumer-based development" that Alvin Toffler predicted in the past has already been realized in the Internet world.

As a matter of fact, this prosumer-based method has moved to an even more advanced stage than what Toffler predicted.

That is, consumers are now participating not only in the "development" process of products and services but also in the "sales" and the "promotion" processes.

For instance, the "Net-based group purchase" system that is now popular in the Internet world.

In this system, a company for instance may offer a "20 % discount for a purchase of 100 counts" through their online shop, and then consumers get together on the Internet to form a group to co-purchase the product, so that they will qualify for the group discount. This is precisely a system where producers and consumers collaborate on "sales promotion" and "purchase promotion"; it is a new method that should be referred to as "prosumer-based sales and purchase promotion."

For another instance, the "affiliate" programs that have been spreading in the Internet world in recent years.

In those programs, consumers for instance may introduce and recommend their favorite products or services on their web sites or blogs, and when the products or services are purchased via those web pages, they are rewarded a certain type of perquisite or benefit such as points. This, in a sense, is a system where producers and consumers collaborate on "promotions" and "marketing"; it is a new marketing practice that should be referred to as "prosumer-based marketing."

Moreover, along with "prosumer-based development," there is another prevalent development method that utilizes the wisdom of consumers and users, which is so-called "open source-based development."

A symbolic instance of this is the earlier-mentioned "Linux Project" where computer engineers worldwide, who are computer users at the same time, gather on the Internet to share their wisdom to develop new operating system. This development method is called "open source-based development" since it is realized by widely and openly collecting the knowledge and the wisdom of consumers and users to incorporate into the development of new products, services, software and concepts.

Likewise, the "grassroots review" service of Amazon, as well as the "grassroots encyclopedia" service of Wikipedia, are created by open contributions of users and therefore can be considered "open source-based services." Additionally, various "Q&A sites" can also be considered "open source-based services" since members of the Net community voluntarily answer other members' questions without compensation.

As illustrated above, in the coming age, consumers will begin to directly "participate" in the design, the development, the production, the sales and the promotion of products and services as they collaborate with or play an alternate role for companies. Thus, the paradigm that should be referred to as "participatory economy" is now about to be born.

In a "participatory economy," consumers and users participate in activities voluntarily without compensation, and therefore its reality is a "hybrid economy," the merging of "monetary economy" and "voluntary economy" discussed in Chapter 5.

"Direct Democracy" of Economies

Will Be Realized

Then, what is occurring here?

What is occurring in "economic principles" as a consequence of the spreading "participatory economy," as represented in "prosumer-based development" and "open source-based services"?

Let us state this simply.

"Direct democracy" of economies is being realized.

This statement may surprise some readers.

However, the market economy up to today has actually been an "indirect democracy."

No matter how businesses in the market economy claim to be "customer-centric" with a focus on "customer satisfaction" and develop products and services that cater to customers' needs and wants, the reality of the economy has no doubt been an "indirect democracy."

Because, just like the way the representative system functions in politics, companies have played a role as representatives of consumers to study and analyze consumers' needs, so as to develop, produce and sell products and services that reflect the needs of as many consumers as possible, capturing the "largest common denominator" so to speak. It has no doubt been an "indirect democracy," since this is just like the way that politicians as representatives of the electorate study and analyze the electorate's needs and wants, so as to realize the policies that reflect the needs and wants of as much electorate as possible, capturing the "largest common denominator."

However, as the Internet revolution advances, this paradigm is beginning to shift.

In the coming age, consumers will begin to participate in the development, the productions and the sales of products and services in the forms of "prosumer-based development" and "open source-based services." This means that the "direct democracy" of economies is being realized.

As illustrated above, the paradigm shift from "beneficiary economy" to "participatory economy" is in a sense a paradigm shift from "indirect democracy" to "direct democracy" in economies. As a matter of fact, the paradigm shift to "participatory economy" is, again, the "spiral development" of Hegel's Dialectic.

Because, in the beginning of the human history, "producers" and "consumers" were not separated. Before "division of labor" and "specialization" developed in societies, "consumers" were the "producers," and "producers" were the "consumers."

In other words, it was an age of "self-sufficiency."

"Participatory economy," in a sense, is a revival of this old and nostalgic age.

But this regression to "participatory economy" is also a "spiral development."

It is not a simple revival of old and nostalgic things.

Each time, it has climbed up "one more spiral step."

Each time, some "new value" has been added.

This "participatory economy" is precisely a "self-sufficient economy" that has become extremely efficient and convenient as a result of the Internet revolution.

And this is only the beginning of the paradigm shift from "beneficiary economy" to "participatory economy."

It will eventually lead a fundamental change in the way of capitalism as well as of societies.

However, many politicians, administrative officials and executives unfortunately have not realized the importance of this paradigm shift.

"Methods of Innovation"

Will Achieve Innovation

Then, why will the paradigm shift to "participatory economy" lead a fundamental change in the way of capitalism as well as of societies?

It is because another important paradigm shift in societies will be led as a result.

What paradigm shift is it?

The paradigm shift of "innovation."

This is what will be led.
In what form?

In the form of the shift from "beneficiary innovation" to "participatory innovation."

That is, innovations in societies up to now have been achieved by such people as exceptionally talented scientists and engineers, aspiring entrepreneurs and executives, and politicians and administrators with outstanding abilities. Many people have only been one-sidedly "benefiting" from those innovations.

However, this paradigm of innovation is beginning to shift.

In the coming age, many people will be actively "participating" in innovation processes. "Prosumer-based development" and "open source-based development" occurring now in the economic field are merely a "prelude" of this paradigm shift.

This movement, which is expressed in such terms as "democratization of innovations," "open innovations" and "user innovations," will become increasingly widespread from now on.

Without needing to quote Joseph Schumpeter's words, innovation is an essential element in the development of capitalism and should never be lost from societies in order that they may permanently progress and develop.

However, the fact is that "innovation" itself is now going through an innovation process.

Then, why is the paradigm shift from "beneficiary innovation" to "participatory innovation" important now? Why is the "democratization of innovation" important?

It is by no means because "When consumers participate in innovations, the development of products and services that satisfy the needs of consumers can be realized." It is not because "The knowledge and wisdom of many people in the society can be utilized in innovations in various fields," either.

Then why is it?

It is because it affects people's "sense of happiness" in the society.

When many people in a society feel a sense of happiness, it is by no means because the society is "ideal." Societies, in a sense, are always "imperfect" and have "problems."

Then why can many people feel a "sense of happiness" in an "imperfect" society?

It must be because, even if the society is currently "imperfect" and has many "problems," they are able to believe that it will change to a "better society" toward the future. If many people in the United States felt a sense of happiness by seeing the rise of President Barack Obama, the reason for this must have been precisely that. If many people in the United States felt a sense of happiness by the rise of President Barack Obama while faced with serious problems, such as the chaos of the War in Iraq, the global economic crisis and the global environmental problems, it must have been because they could believe that "The United States will change for the better," just as his word "Change!"

People's sense of happiness will become even greater under a certain situation.

What is the situation?

It is when people are "participating" in making changes in the society.

Under a situation like this, people's sense of happiness will be heightened even more. Even if a society is imperfect and has many problems, people can feel a great sense of happiness when they feel that they are participating in activities to "change the society for the better."

This must have been why President Obama received people's overwhelming support during the election campaign.

He did not simply say the word "Change!"

He did say the words "We can change!"
That is, "We can change the society with our strength!"
That message moved a number of people.

This is why.
This is why the paradigm shift of "innovation" is important.
The paradigm shift from the innovation in which people only "benefit," to the innovation in which many people "participate."
This is what is important.

"Democracy" Will Also Achieve

Spiral Development

This paradigm shift of "innovation" is, in other words, the "democratization of innovation."
Actually, as this movement spreads, a large-scale regression to the origin will occur in societies.
What regression?

"Democracy's" regression to the origin.

This is what will occur.
What does it mean?
There are three kinds of regression to the origin in democracy.

The first regression to the origin is from the democracy of "politics" to the democracy of "economies" and "cultures."
Up to the present, we have unconsciously assumed that "democracy" means "a matter in politics." However, democracy in fact is not a matter limited to the domain of "politics." It is a matter that is fundamentally associated with activities in the whole society, including "economies" and "cultures." Weather or not people can

participate in the activities of the whole society is precisely the fundamental subject of "democracy."

Then, due to the first regression to the origin, the second regression to the origin will naturally occur.

The second regression to the origin is from the participation in "decision-making" to the participation in "social changes."

Since the notion of democracy has been primarily discussed in terms of "politics" up to now, we have unconsciously assumed that democracy means for people to participate in "decision-making in the society." This is symbolized in the term "representative system." This term, which means that some people "represent" others, symbolizes our assumption.

However, true democracy does not simply mean that many people participate in the "decision-making in the society." It essentially means that many people participate in "making changes in the society." The meaning and significance of this has been discussed earlier.

The third regression to the origin is from "indirect democracy" to "direct democracy."

When presented with this statement, many readers may wonder: "Does it mean that the kind of direct democracy where anybody can freely present his or her opinions on various policies through the Internet will be realized?"

However, please remember once again the first and the second regressions to the origin. As has just been stated, democracy is not only a matter of the domain of "politics," but it is a matter of very extensive domains including "economies" and "cultures." In addition, true democracy does not mean for people to simply participate in the "decision-making in the society," but it means for people to participate in "making changes in the society."

Therefore, "democracy's" regression to the origin, namely the regression to "direct democracy" that will occur from now, precisely means the emergence of direct democracy that has climbed up one step higher and has achieved "spiral development" in both of those senses described above.

Now the paradigm shift from "beneficiary economy" to "participatory economy" has been explored in this chapter. As has been discussed, the old and nostalgic economic principle of "participatory economy" in fact contains an extremely important meaning that is associated with enhancing people's sense of happiness in the society.

And, clear philosophy and deep thought on "people's sense of happiness" are precisely what are required in the fifth paradigm shift, which is to be discussed in the next chapter.

Then, what is the fifth paradigm shift?

Chapter 7

The Paradigm Shift
from "Unlimited Growth Economy"
to "Global Environment Economy"

The Age When We Should Be Prepared for

"Limited Economy"

The paradigm shift from "unlimited growth economy" to "global environment economy."

This is the fifth paradigm shift.

In other words, this is the shift from "unlimited economy" to "limited economy."

This is what will occur.

The reason for this is clear.

Needless to say, the global environmental problems that human society is currently faced with are explicitly teaching us, in a very serious manner, how the global space, energy and natural resources are "limited."

This is a fact that many people around the world are already aware of.

What conveyed this fact to us in a clear message, backed with a vast amount of the most recent data on global environmental changes, were the publication *An Inconvenient Truth* authored by the former Vice President of the United States Albert Gore and the documentary film of the same title that was produced based on the publication.

The film won the 2007 Academy Award for Best Documentary Feature, and Albert Gore was recognized for his devoted activities to address global environmental problems, which led him to win the 2007 Nobel Peace Prize.

However, the "limitedness" of the global space, energy and natural resources were in fact already stated in 1972 in a very shocking manner.

It was presented in a publication called *The Limits to Growth*.

Subtitled *A Report for the Club of Rome's Project on the Predicament of Mankind* and published by the world-recognized think tank the Club of Rome, this report was based on the future prediction conducted by a team of researchers including Dennis Meadows, then a professor at the Massachusetts Institute of Technology, and Donella Meadows, then an assistant professor at Dartmouth College. It gave a devastating shock to the entire world at that time.

That is because their future predictions which utilized a global simulation model indicated that the economic growth of the humankind as a whole would reach its limit within one hundred years due to the following five problems: population explosion, food shortages, resource depletion, energy crisis and environmental pollution.

In other words, the alarm for the "limitedness" of the global space, energy and natural resources was already sounded in 1972.

However, even though it has been nearly four decades since the alarm was sounded, the current economics is still caught in the "unlimited growth" paradigm and has been able to produce neither theories nor methods for discussing economies that assume the "limitedness."

Moreover, the current economics is still caught in the "unlimited growth economy" paradigm; many corporate executives still continue to eagerly pursue "increase in sales and profits," and many nations still continue to eagerly pursue "increase in GDP."

Everyone is already aware of this fact:

Realizing "unlimited" economic growth is nothing but an illusion.

This is a fact that everyone is aware of.

Nevertheless, the current economics has not yet been able to produce new economic theories that assume "limited space" and "limited resources."

However, that is natural in a sense.

Because, what are required now are "paradigm shifts."

Not simply "reframing economic theories," but "paradigm shifts in economic principles."

If what are required are "paradigm shifts," we cannot see the new paradigm as long as we stay within the old paradigm. We cannot see the new world with old glasses.

Then, what kind is this new paradigm?

What kind is the "global environment economy" paradigm that assumes "limited space" and "limited resources"?

The answer cannot be stated simply, however, there is an interesting term that suggests the direction toward which "global environment economy" should move.

"GNH."

That is the term.

It represents "Gross National Happiness."

Advocated in a small Asian country Bhutan, the notion of GNH is quietly starting to spread to the world, as symbolized by the fact that a session at the 2009 Davos Conference called "From GDP to Gross National Happiness" attracted popularity.

Although the index of GNH has not established its position as a concrete concept or a theory, it provides us with an important viewpoint that will help us accomplish future paradigm shifts in economic principles.

Because, for those of us who are caught in an old paradigm, the term GNH itself has an impact that will lead us to switch our way of thinking.

In the method of creative thinking, we should deeply engrave the following words in our minds:

Do not try to devise the "design of the bridge."
Try to devise "ways to cross the river."

Just as these words suggest, we typically think of creating a bridge at first for the purpose of crossing a river, but once we begin designing the bridge, our minds are caught concentrating on the design itself, becoming oblivious to the fact that our true purpose is to "cross the river." Then we forget that there are various other ways to cross the river, such as ships, tunnels, airplanes and swimming, thus becoming to believe that "bridging the river" is the only way to cross it.

This metaphor can be applied to economics. The idea of economics was originally born for the purpose of realizing happiness for many people, and as a method for realizing happiness, we have been pursuing "economic growth." However, current economics has strangely become to assume that "economic growth" is the only way that can make people happy, although it is merely "one of the means" for realizing happiness.

As the global environmental problems worsen, many of us are beginning to question the simple formula of "economic growth =

happiness," but nevertheless, we are still caught in this old paradigm.

On the other hand, the term GNH contains a word in itself that literally indicates our ultimate goal. It is the word "happiness." Therefore, if we focus on this word in our discussions, we will never fall in the pitfall of "forgetting about crossing the river and being caught in the design of the bridge."

What Is the New "Index of Wealth"?

Now, what can we do to enhance GNH?
How can we enhance nations' "degree of happiness"?

This also is a fundamental question that cannot be fully discussed in one book, but I have a suggestion to make here.

We should stop evaluating "wealth" only within the paradigm of "monetary economy."

Then, what is the "wealth" that goes beyond the paradigm of "monetary economy" and that cannot be evaluated by the measure of "currency"?

This is actually what we have been discussing up to this point through the previous five chapters.

We have been discussing the "five paradigm shifts" that will occur in economic principles as well as the five new paradigms. We have also been discussing the "five values" that are emphasized in each of the new paradigms.

Complexity Economy: A society wherein people value ethical sense and codes of conduct in individuals and companies.

Empathy Economy: A society wherein people can share knowledge and wisdom freely through their empathy.

Voluntary Economy: A society wherein people practice positive activities through their goodwill and affection and thus obtain "satisfaction of mind."

Participatory Economy: A society wherein people can freely participate in social innovations and social changes.

Global Environment Economy: A society wherein people can live with nature and maintain its sustainability.

However, when we discuss these "values," readers may immediately present the following question:

"I understand that those values are important. But, how can we evaluate those values by an "objective measure"?

In response to this question, I would like to clearly answer:

It is this way of thinking that needs to be altered.

The way of thinking whereby we simply assume "Things that cannot be evaluated by objective measures are worthless" when discussing social values. Isn't it the way of thinking itself that is the problem with us?

We need to realize the fact that there is a serious misunderstanding behind this way of thinking.

The idea of "objective measures."

What has been brought about as a consequence of evaluating values in society for instance by a single objective measure called "currency"? Due to this way of evaluating values, haven't we lost the ability to recognize "diverse values" in society from a diverse range of viewpoints? Isn't it this "simplification of evaluation measures" that has caused the "simplification of value systems" and "simplification of cultures" in society? Aren't "diverse values" referred to as "diverse values" because they cannot be evaluated by a single measure?

In this age when the world is moving toward "pluralism" where people acknowledge the "diverse values" of each other in order for various nations and ethnic groups to co-exist, we need to realize the fact that only the field of economics has not yet shifted to the theoretical system that assumes "diverse values."

What is "maturity of cultures"?

This was discussed in Chapter 4.

"Mature cultures" are the ones that consider "invisible values."

This is what was discussed.

If so, in order for capitalism to mature in the coming age, we will need to reconsider our habit of applying "currency" as "a single measure to evaluate diverse values." We should reconsider our habit of easily applying the measure of currency based only on the reason that using the measure can lead to easier consensus-building and hassle-free convenience.

Then, if we are to aim at applying "diverse measures to evaluate diverse values," what kinds of methods are there for us?

Methods for Evaluating Diverse Values

by Diverse Measures

As a matter of fact, methods for these are now being born.

They are being born in the Internet world.

In many of the Net communities, diverse evaluations of products and services are made and presented in various different ways. For instance, in the book reviews at the Amazon website, in addition to "quantitative evaluation" based on the scale of one-to-five stars, diverse evaluations made by each reviewer are presented "as is" in their unique writing style. For another instance, in the blog world that is now rapidly expanding, there is a method spreading by which bloggers who share similar values connect with each other through trackbacks so that they can base their decision-making and actions on other bloggers' comments.

As seen above, methods for evaluating diverse values from diverse viewpoints without forcefully applying a single measure are spreading in the Internet world, although they are still at a quite primitive stage. In other words, the Internet world is not moving toward the direction that creates "a single quantitative measure" for evaluating diverse values.

It is most likely that new methods will be born beyond this movement in the Internet world.

More methods, by which diverse values can be evaluated from diverse viewpoints without impairing the diversity, will be born.

This is because the Internet world in its essence possesses a culture that embraces "diversity." Just as the proverb "As the boy, so the man" may apply, the Internet world possesses a deeply-engraved "culture of diversity" with which "simplified" methods such as "evaluation by the measure of currency" and "evaluation by a quantitative measure" are not compatible.

Additionally, in decision-making discussions in society, we tend to lean toward "majority vote" and "the greatest good for the greatest number," but when we reflect on the history of humankind, there are quite a few instances where a community embraces a culture of "continuing discussions until participants' opinions are settled."

We need to recognize the fact that cultures where decisions are mostly based on a prompt "majority vote" are also unusual conditions created by the modern society where streamlining, rationalization and acceleration have been sought after.

When we reflect on the long history of humankind, we become to realize that what we consider "common sense" in the modern society had not at all been "common sense" in the past.

And, if we understand the dialectic development in our history, then we realize that old things revive with new values and meanings.

For certain, the "old and nostalgic wisdom" that was cultivated through the history of humankind is now reviving in this modern society.

Its "spiral development."
Its "spiral staircase."
What will we see beyond this spiral staircase?

When we turn our eyes to the future beyond, we will be able to see the deep value of Japanese style management and Japanese style capitalism that have been considered obsolete, by casting a new light on them.

Let us discuss this subject, entering into the next chapter

Chapter 8

The Japanese Style Management

Which Has Embodied

"Corporate Ethics"

Why Will the "Nostalgic Value System"

Revive?

Through the previous chapters, I have explained the "five paradigm shifts" that will occur in economic principles.

And I have stated that capitalism will achieve "five evolutions" as a result of those paradigm shifts.

Now, let us review those five paradigm shifts below:

The shift from "operationalism economy" to "complexity economy."

The shift from "knowledge economy" to "empathy economy."

The shift from "monetary economy" to "voluntary economy."

The shift from "beneficiary economy" to "participatory economy."

The shift from "unlimited growth economy" to "global environment economy."

However, readers in Japan who have read up to this point may be feeling a slight sense of surprise.

Because, the "new value systems" that those paradigm shifts require of companies or societies give us Japanese a somewhat nostalgic feeling.

The reason for this is clear.

It is because those "new value systems" are precisely the value systems that were emphasized in Japanese style management and that underlay Japanese style capitalism.

From here on, I will discuss this subject by introducing the "uniqueness of Japanese style management."

To accomplish this, I will dedicate Chapters 8 through 12 to the discussion of five unique features of Japanese style management, as described below:

(1) The management which has embodied
    "corporate ethics"
(2) The management which has recognized
    "invisible capital"
(3) The management which has unified
    "social contribution" and "pursuit of profits"
(4) The management which has pursued
    the "unification of subject and object"
(5) The management which has assumed
    "*yugen*" (limitedness),"*mujo*" (impermanence) and
    "*jinen*" (living as nature)

The Japanese Style Management

Which Has Embodied "CSR"

since the Old Days

To begin with, "complexity economy" in the first paradigm shift.

It can also be referred to as "butterfly economy." As described in the metaphor "When a butterfly flutters its wings in Beijing, a hurricane occurs in New York," a slight fluctuation born at the corner of a market can cause dramatic and enormous changes in the entire market. The best prescription for coping with this economy that has acquired new properties was already mentioned.

The self-discipline of each company.

Specifically, the ethical sense of executives who lead the company.

That is the most important point, as discussed.

In this sense, the fact that both Western and Japanese companies are moving toward the direction of emphasizing "CSR" (Corporate Social Responsibility) and "social contribution" through reflecting on various corporate scandals can be seen as a major evolution of capitalism.

As discussed in Chapter 3, the International Organization for Standardization (ISO) has established international standards for CSR to propose implementation of the concept in companies worldwide, thus creating a worldwide trend of CSR.

However, if we are to open-mindedly look back on the history of "Japanese style management" and "Japanese style capitalism" without being fixed on this worldwide trend, then we will realize that the thought of CSR in fact has been firmly established there since very long ago.

For instance, the words expressed by Eiichi Shibusawa, a businessman in early 1900s: "An abacus in our right hand, the Analects of Confucius in our left hand."

For another instance, the admonition of the Sumitomo Zaibatsu (financial group): "No pursuit for easy money."

For yet another instance, the philosophy of merchants in the Omi region: "The 'three goods': the good for the seller, the good for the buyer and the good for society."

These words have been openly expressed in Japan.

That is, as symbolized in these words, the nation of Japan has held the established thought of emphasizing companies' social responsibility and social contribution since very long ago.

More importantly, in Japan, the notions of social responsibility and social contribution did not simply mean an "activity forced by law" or a "social duty," but they rather meant an "autonomy" and a "voluntary mission." In other words, the notions of social responsibility and social contribution existed in Japan as a part of "a sense of ethics and values in each individual," "organizational climate" and "social cultures."

For instance, the Japanese word "*hataraku*" means "the act of working." In fact, "*hata*" means "neighbors" and "*raku*" means "happiness." Therefore, in Japan "working" literally means "for neighbors' happiness." In other words, the view that "work" is an act of realizing happiness for other people and for the world has been passed down in Japan. Moreover, this "view of work" has been naturally ingrained not only among the limited number of elites but also among ordinary people.

Furthermore, the English word "labor" has a connotation of "toil," while the Japanese word "*hataraku*" does not. As this Japanese word may suggest, unlike Western nations, Japan has not held the thought of "early retirement" where a successful life means to be free from the burden of labor at a younger age and to lead a leisurely life. Many people in Japan, rather than wishing for an "early retirement," have had the ingrained view of work where they wish to "serve a useful purpose for the world as long as they are healthy" even after their age-limit retirement.

This thought is also a component of the Japanese "view of occupation" where they consider one's occupation to be a "divine vocation" and where they consider it precious, regardless of the type of occupation, to pursue it with a sense of mission to "do good for the world and people." This view of occupation by each individual has also been incorporated into company organizations as a climate to value the thought expressed in the words by the

Japanese Buddist monk Saichō, "If you light up a small corner of society, you are society's treasure," and this climate has further reinforced the individuals' view of occupation.

Moreover, what is behind the reason for companies and individuals in Japan to abide by laws and to be ethical is not the thought that "We will be punished if we don't abide by laws" but the culture of being aware of "*sekensama*" (the world and people), the thought that "Even if we may be forgiven by laws, we will not be forgiven by the world."

Just as Ruth Benedict pointed out in her insights presented in her writing *The Chrysanthemum and the Sword*, the behavioral principles of the Japanese people are based on the culture where they discipline themselves through the fear of "shame," not through the fear of "guilt." This culture in a sense can be viewed as one where people embrace "aesthetics" and "sense of beauty" as their behavioral principles.

As illustrated above, the notions of social responsibility and social contribution have existed in Japan not simply as an "activity forced by law" or a "social duty" but as an "autonomy" and a "voluntary mission," and furthermore, as a part of "individuals' sense of ethics and values," "organizational climate" and "social cultures."

In this sense, in Japan, the thought of CSR has existed as a deep thought that is embodied into corporate culture.

The "Third Way" Which Is

neither "Noninterference" nor "Control"

On the other hand, the recent trend of worldwide CSR was born through reflecting on the past corporate scandals such as those of Enron and WorldCom, taking the viewpoint of how to regulate global capitalism that had gone "too extreme." Although such a viewpoint is certainly important, this trend of CSR, due to its "roots," possesses a risk that may lead the notion of CSR to be interpreted in a distorted way.

This fact has already been discussed in Chapter 3.

That is, even the notion of CSR has been placed in the context of "market principles" and thus has fallen into a "passive thought" expressed as follows: "We place emphasis on CSR because otherwise we won't be able to survive in the competitive market," and "We place emphasis on CSR because otherwise we will lose shareholders' support."

As discussed earlier, this is what we should call the distortion of the thought of CSR by global capitalism.

In other words, in global capitalism, everything has been placed in the context of "market principles" and the "principles of competition" to "survive" and to "become the winner" in the market. And now, even the thought of CSR is being placed within "market principles" and the "principles of competition," despite the fact that the thought was born for correcting the courses of "market principles" and the "principles of competition" that had gone wrong and too extreme.

Let us confirm this important matter:

The idea that "We don't do this because it is against the law" always possesses a risk of easily falling into the opposite idea that "We may do this if it isn't against the law."

Likewise, the idea that "We don't do this because we can't survive in the competitive market" always possesses the risk of instantly falling into the opposite idea that "We may do this if we can survive in the competitive market."

Therefore, CSR in its essence should be naturally fulfilled in the absence of outside forces, based on the executives' sense of ethics and values and as a part of corporate philosophy and cultures.

Why has global capitalism reached its limit?

The reason must be that it has fallen into the most dangerous pitfall that is hidden behind the thought of "market principles."

That is, the "market principle" that is defined as "realizing advanced economies and societies by utilizing human desire."

It is true that this "market principle" has enabled economic prosperity and social innovations up to the present time, but we have been so fascinated by its success that we have unconditionally depended on it.

As a consequence, we have come to the point where it is impossible to control "human desire," which in its essence is supposed to be "utilized." That is the ultimate cause of the current subprime crisis.

Then, how can we control "human desire"?

In order to accomplish that, it may be necessary to establish "laws" and tighten "regulations."

However, there are two problems with these methods.

The first is that tightening regulations hinders free competition in markets.

The second is that, despite tightened laws and regulations, there will always be people who find a loophole to pursue what they wish.

This is precisely the reason that capitalism should learn a method different from "noninterference" and "control"; what it should learn is the third method, "autonomy."

Then, is "autonomy" a method that is possible to be accomplished?

The "View of Humans" on Which

Japanese Style Management Has Been Based

"It is impossible to accomplish autonomy.

Even if we expect a sense of ethics from corporate executives and employees, humans, as is their nature, are susceptible to their weakness.

This is precisely why laws should be strictly enforced."

Readers may raise this kind of argument based on the "view of human nature as inherently evil."

A sad age when this view of humans is somehow very convincing.

We have witnessed so many cases where corporate executives and employees have gone too extreme and off the right path.

However, with this reality in mind, let us confirm another important matter:

Institutions that are formed based on a certain view of humans, as they take root in society, in return increase the number of people to whom those institutions apply.

We should realize how dreadful this paradox is.

When we take a long-term viewpoint, institutions that are based on the "view of human nature as inherently evil" will by no means be an influence to enhance our qualities as humans.

Then, is it the case that we are not able to base the "view of human nature as inherently good" and expect corporate executives and employees to act based on their good ethical sense?

As a matter of fact, this exact way of corporate management existed in the past.

In the Japanese style management of the past, this way of management was realized.

However, it was not realized through a simple method of requiring executives and employees to act based on their good "ethical sense."

If the executives and employees under the past Japanese style management had a strong grip on good "sense of ethics," it was realized not due to "education of mind" but due to "corporate cultures."

If so, what kinds of corporate cultures are they?

They are symbolized by the way that Japanese companies perceive "CSR." That is, the way they perceive "social responsibility" and "social contribution."

Amid the worldwide trend of CSR, many companies around the world use the term "social responsibility," but they mostly use it to mean "compliance with laws" and "corporate ethics." They mean that they will abide by laws and maintain corporate ethics.

In other words, many companies around the world use the term "social responsibility" to mean "not doing wrong to society."

However, to Japanese companies, "social responsibility" did not carry a non-active and passive meaning as in a simple sense of "not doing wrong to society." It precisely meant to actively and positively "do good to society."

Simply stated, the term "social responsibility," to Japanese companies, was synonymous to "social contribution."

There is another thing to be mentioned.

Japanese companies had a culture where they stress social responsibility to their employees by using a more wonderful word than "responsibility" or "duty."

What is the word?

"Mission."

That is the word.

In Japanese companies, employees have not been taught to "pursue the responsibility and duties to deliver flawless products to the customer," but they have been taught to "pursue the mission to deliver flawless products to the customer."

The words "responsibility" and "duty" seem to be similar to the word "mission" in their meaning, but they are actually not the same. The words "responsibility" and "duty" contain the negative nuance that one must pursue these concepts because otherwise he or she will be "accused" or "punished," while the word "mission" contains the positive nuance that one will receive "fulfillment of mind as a reward" when it is accomplished.

This is the important meaning of the "view of humans."

When corporate executives work with employees, what kind of mindset should they be promoting?

This must be the crucial matter.

Should they be promoting the mindset of "avoiding accusation," or the mindset of "doing good"? This is precisely the point that clearly determines whether humans should be viewed as "inherently evil" or "inherently good."

The problem with the "ethical sense" of executives and employees, which the current capitalism is faced with.

There exists a profound paradox regarding the "sense of ethics" itself.

Let us state this simply.

The true sense of ethics is not to be cultivated through teaching "not to do wrong."

The true sense of ethics is to be naturally acquired as a result of being taught "to do good" and thus gaining a heightened level of humanity.

This is where we find the essence of the "sense of ethics" problem with executives and employees that the current capitalism is faced with.

As a matter of fact, encouraging executives and employees just by stressing "duty" and "responsibility" of "not doing wrong to society" cannot heighten their sense of ethics.

The right way to truly heighten their sense of ethics is to urge them to "do good to society" and promote their sense of mission. This is because people who have a thought to do good and to contribute to society will naturally not think of doing wrong to society.

In other words, this matter is about cultivating corporate cultures where social contribution is valued. Although this seems to be a circuitous route, it is actually the best method for realizing compliance with laws in companies and maintaining corporate ethics.

In this exact sense, in the Japanese style management of the past, social contribution was considered to be the most important factor.

For instance, the following words have been clearly mentioned in Japanese style management:

"A company contributes to society through its main business."

Any Japanese person would recognize these words and understand the meaning. As symbolized in these words, in Japanese style management, the notion of social contribution was deeply ingrained into "corporate cultures." Therefore, the notion of "corporate ethics" was also embodied in Japanese style management.

The words "A company contributes to society through its main business" in Japanese style management.

These simple words are what captured far in advance the future paradigm shifts in capitalism as well as the new value systems toward which the future capitalism of the world will move.

This will be discussed in detail in Chapter 10.

However, before entering into this subject, there is another important matter that needs to be discussed.

It is regarding the "view of reward" in Japanese style management.

Because, the second paradigm shift to "empathy economy" will actually lead the "view of reward" that has been valued in Japanese style management.

Chapter 9

The Japanese Style Management
Which Has Recognized
"Invisible Capital"

Today's Corporate Executives
Who Have Lost Sight of "Invisible Capital"

Now, what again is the second paradigm shift to "empathy economy"?

As seen in Chapter 4, "knowledge economy" will go through a paradigm shift to "empathy economy," and in order to cope with this new "empathy economy," we need to place the most emphasis on the kind of capital that should be referred to as "empathy capital."

"Empathy capital" means the "invisible capital" of the following types:

> Knowledge Capital
> Relation Capital
> Trust Capital
> Brand Capital
> Culture Capital

In "empathy economy," corporate executives are required to acquire the ability to evaluate these types of "invisible capital" and to expand it.

However, despite the fact that it has been quite long since we entered the age of "knowledge economy" and "empathy economy," there unfortunately have not been very many executives who place emphasis on evaluating and expanding "invisible capital."

The primary cause of this lies in the standard for evaluating companies in global capitalism.

In spite of the fact that these types of "invisible capital" are increasing in importance, evaluations of companies in the stock market are still mostly based on the "visible numbers" that appear in financial statements.

As a consequence, executives in many of the listed companies are caught focusing on the "immediate numbers," thus leading to a biased way of management from a short-term and a constricted perspective.

This fact has already been pointed out by a number of intellects. There have been many criticisms where they note that the global capitalism which is heavily dependent on market principles is causing a big problem in the courses of development of new technologies, long-term human resource development, cultivation of positive corporate cultures and establishing relationships of trust with consumers.

Thus, the reality that the evaluations of companies are still mostly based on "visible numbers" is creating various problems, and therefore excellent executives have no other way but to incorporate a "double standard" in their management of companies.

For instance, they work to avoid shareholders' criticisms by demonstrating to the stock market and analysts the company's emphasis on policies for increasing sales and profits, while within the company they continuously implement policies to develop new technologies, to nurture human resources from a long-term perspective, to cultivate positive corporate cultures and to establish trusted relationships with consumers.

In other words, an ironic situation has been created in the realm of global capitalism where the more able an executive, the more he or she is forced to employ "double standards" and to be of "dual personality" in order to cope with both the stock market and internal matters.

Maturity Means to Become Able to See "Invisible Values"

On the other hand, the subprime crisis has opened an opportunity to reflect on the ways of a management style that focus on short-term numbers, and thus the importance of taking a longer-term perspective in management is now being recognized.

Then what can corporate executives do in order to evaluate and expand such kinds of "invisible capital" as knowledge capital, relation capital, trust capital, brand capital and culture capital that are increasing in importance in "empathy economy"?

As a matter of fact, in the Japanese style management of the past, it was considered an important role for corporate executives to evaluate and expand these types of "invisible capital."

This is because excellent executives in the Japanese companies of the past valued the following elements:

"Sparkle in employees' eyes," "Employees' joy of working,"
"Climate and atmosphere in the workplace,"
"Harmony of employees," "Corporate culture,"
"Empathy with customers," "Trust from society,"
"Reputation in the world."

In the past, excellent executives in Japanese companies placed importance on these "invisible values." These values do not appear in "financial statements," however, the types of values that are not reflected in "visible numbers" are what excellent Japanese executives used to deeply consider.

Moreover, there was another factor aside from the existence of those "executives" that was wonderful about the past Japanese style management.

It is the fact that "managers" and "employees" in Japanese companies also placed importance on "invisible values."

This is symbolized by the "view of reward" in Japanese style management.

Namely, what is "reward for work"?

This "view of reward" was where the strength of Japanese style management resided.

Because, in Japanese style management, managers and employees placed importance not only on "visible rewards" but also on "invisible rewards."

"Visible rewards" are, needless to say, "salaries or annual pay" and "high positions or status."

Then what are "invisible rewards"?

As a matter of fact, in Japanese style management, many company employees have felt that the following four factors are also important rewards for work.

The first is "joy of working."

In Japanese workplaces, it has often been mentioned that "The reward for work is the work itself." These are wonderful words that carry various meanings, and in one, it means that "The reward for work is the joy of working itself."

Then what is "joy of working"?

It by no means is to "receive higher pay" or to "climb the corporate ladder faster."

As mentioned earlier, in Japan, to work ("*hataraku*") means "for neighbors' happiness." Therefore, "joy of working" is precisely the joy of realizing happiness for somebody or for the world. In the Japanese companies of the past, this kind of joy certainly existed.

The second is the "ability as a professional."
In the Japanese workplaces of the past, employees always felt the "joy of polishing their skills."
It is different from the now-common ideas of "upskilling for more salaries" and "improving skills to enhance one's marketability."
In Japan, a value system has existed where people view "polishing skills" itself as the joy of and the reward for work.
This value system is reflected in the words once mentioned by Ichiro Suzuki, a baseball player in the U.S. Major League Baseball.

At the end of a season when he had set a single-season major league record with 262 hits, he was asked the following question by the media:
"Ichiro-san, what is your next goal?"
His answer to the question was this:
"Yes, to become better at baseball."

As symbolized by this episode, in Japan, "polishing skills" itself has been considered the joy of and the reward for work.
Additionally, the Japanese people have had the spirit of turning any type of work into "*dō*" (path to the summit of profession). A culture has existed where they turn everything into an art of profession and feel the joy of "polishing skills," which is not limited to such established forms of arts as *ken-dō* (Japanese fencing), *ju-dō* (self-defense martial arts), *sa-dō* (tea ceremony) and *ka-dō* (flower arrangement), but also in such areas as management ("*keiei-dō*"), sales ("*eigyo-dō*"), cooking ("*ryori-dō*"), and even cleaning ("*soji-dō*").

The third is "growth as a human being."
In Japanese companies, just as the words "We polish ourselves

through work" are respected, work has been considered not merely a way of earning a living but a precious occasion to grow as a human being. Therefore, the hardships and difficulties people face at work are culturally considered not "unfortunate troubles" in a simple sense but are "trials" given by Heaven so that they can grow as a human being. This culture is symbolized in the words often mentioned by retiring older employees at a setting such as a farewell party when they have reached their age-limit retirement: "During my service with the company in the past few decades, I have really had rewarding hardships. Owing to everyone, I was able to grow as a human being."

As seen above, in Japanese companies, there existed a culture where "growth as a human being" is considered one of the greatest rewards for work.

The fourth is "encountering companions at the workplace."

In Japan, the proverb "A chance acquaintance is a divine ordinance" has been often mentioned, and many people have liked to use the words "*enishi*" (destined relationships) to express their encounters with people. Thus, people in Japanese companies have had a clear sense that co-workers are not just a functional group of people but are "companions who work at the same workplace because they are somehow destined to do so." Therefore, people in Japanese companies have culturally considered it precious to work together as one team and one mind with companions at the workplace to give their best and thus to deepen their destined relationships.

In this sense, in Japanese companies, it has been considered that "encountering companions at the workplace" is also a wonderful reward for work.

As illustrated above, what have been considered important rewards for work in Japanese style management are not only "visible rewards" such as "salaries or annual pay" and "high positions or status," but also "invisible rewards" such as "joy of working," "ability as a professional," "growth as a human being" and "encountering companions at the workplace."

I have discussed this subject in detail in my books: *What is the Reward of Working?*; *The Philosophy of Work*; available in Japanese.

The "View of Reward" and

the "View of Organization"

in Japanese Style Management

Furthermore, in Japanese style management, various "invisible values" other than these "invisible rewards" have also been emphasized.

For instance, in the "view of organization" in Japanese style management.

As stated earlier, people in Japanese companies have had a clear sense that co-workers are not just a functional group of people but are "companions who work at the same workplace because they are somehow destined to do so." At the same time, they have had a sense that what leads them to accomplish work at the workplace is not their personal ability but the support offered behind their activities by their companions. Therefore, at workplaces in Japanese companies, the "harmony of people" and "support for each other" have been highly valued. This is reflected in the word "*okagesama*" (all owing to you) that the Japanese people say when a task has been successfully accomplished, and also in the word "*otagaisama*" (same with us) that they say in response to the words given by their companions as an appreciation for their cooperation.

In other words, "invisible values" such as intangible cooperation and encouragement by companions have been valued also in the "view of organization" in Japanese style management.

Moreover, invisible things have been valued and incorporated also into the "view of communication" in Japanese style management. This is symbolized in the often-used Japanese expressions that translate to "Heart-to-heart communication" and "Eyes are as eloquent as the tongue."

Furthermore, in the "view of education" in Japanese style management, conveying "wisdom inexpressible in words" has been emphasized rather than conveying "knowledge expressible in words," as symbolized in the often-used Japanese expressions that translate to "Learning through your body," "Learning through your breathing" and "Seeing once is more valuable than hearing one hundred times."

In recent years, as study on knowledge management advances in Western nations, the concept of "tacit knowing" presented by Michael Polanyi has been in the spotlight. However, in Japanese style management, passing down and sharing "wisdom inexpressible in words" have been considered valuable since far in advance of the time when the discussions on tacit knowing started in the Western world. This is also reflected in the fact that there tacitly exist "master-and-apprentice" relationships at workplaces in Japanese companies. For instance, excellent professionals in Japanese companies can almost always point to a person and say, "That person is who taught me as my master."

As illustrated above, a culture that recognizes and values "invisible things" has been cultivated in Japanese style management through its long history.

In Chapter 4, we discussed that "Maturity means to become able to see invisible things," and in this sense, Japanese style management has already had the most mature thought in the world.

This is the age when the paradigm shift to "knowledge economy" and then to "empathy economy" is about to occur.

In this age, what is required of companies worldwide is to recognize, to value and to expand "invisible value" and "invisible capital."

Therefore, in the coming age, the value systems that were clearly valued in the past Japanese style management will be sought after again.

Then, what about the third paradigm shift to "voluntary economy"?

As a matter of fact, there also will be a revival of a value system of Japanese style management in this paradigm shift.

This is what we will discuss next.

Chapter 10

The Japanese Style Management
Which Has Unified
"Social Contribution" and
"Pursuit of Profit"

How Should We Cope with the Contradiction of

"Social Contribution" and "Pursuit of Profit"?

The third paradigm shift is from "monetary economy" to "voluntary economy."

What kind of paradigm shift is this again?

Let us review it below.

Society up to the present has been overwhelmingly dominated by the economic principle called "monetary economy." This is an economy where people conduct activities for the purpose of "acquisition of money."

However, the Internet revolution that happened in the mid 1990s caused "voluntary economy," which had been placed in the position of a "shadow economy," to rapidly increase in impact. "Voluntary economy" refers to an economy where people conduct activities for the purpose of "satisfaction of mind."

When looked from the viewpoint of Hegel's Dialectic, this is a revival of the old and nostalgic voluntary economy through "spiral development." Using this same viewpoint, we can foresee that what will happen next is the "interpenetration of opposing objects." That is, monetary economy and voluntary economy, which appear to be two opposing economic principles, will merge into one, and thus the new economic principle that should be referred to as "hybrid economy" will be born.

This is the paradigm shift that is beginning to occur.

This merging process of monetary economy and voluntary economy, as stated in Chapter 5, is already being realized in markets. In the Internet world, there have already been many specific instances of this merging, such as the grassroots review of the Amazon website, the business model of Google, and the businesses born around Linux.

Then, in what way is this merging process to "hybrid economy" occurring in the actual business world?

This was also discussed earlier in two specific instances.

One is the trend of "CSR" (Corporate Social Responsibility).
The other is the trend of "social entrepreneurship."

In other words, the trend of CSR is in a sense a movement where "voluntary economy" is incorporated into "monetary economy," while the trend of "social entrepreneurship" is a movement where "monetary economy" is incorporated into "voluntary economy."

To state more specifically, the trend of CSR is a movement where "for-profit companies" not only aim at "pursuit of profits" but also place emphasis on "social contribution," while the trend of social entrepreneurship is a movement where "non-profit organizations" work to earn "profits" from their operations of social contribution themselves in order to secure a long-term sustainability of the operations.

That is, when viewed at the company level or organizational level, both the trend of CSR and the trend of social entrepreneurship are precisely the movements where "pursuit of profit" and "social contribution," which have been regarded as two opposing notions, are being unified.

The "Three Expressions" Which Symbolize

Japanese Style Management

However, the fact that the merging of "pursuit of profit" and "social contribution" began conversely means that "pursuit of profit" and "social contribution" have been perceived in the Western world as two opposing notions.

In Japan, however, that has not been the case.

"Pursuit of profit" and "social contribution," which have been perceived as dichotomic notions in the Western world, have always been perceived in the thought of Japanese style management as a unified whole.

This fact is symbolized in the following three expressions that have been mentioned in Japanese style management since the old days:

"A company contributes to society through its main business."

"Profits are the proof that a company has contributed to society."

"The fact that a company makes a large profit represents a call of the people to use this profit to make further contributions to society."

These expressions are of the kind that Japanese companies should proudly present to the world.

Because, these expressions provide a clear answer to the following two fundamental questions:

"What does social contribution mean to companies?"
"What does profit mean to companies?"

The third expression in particular holds a strong influence that can halt the hesitation of corporate executives.

That is because the third expression clearly determines which of the following two the "ultimate purpose" of companies is: "pursuit of profit" or "social contribution."

The ultimate "purpose" of companies is, no doubt, social contribution.
And profits are a "means" to realize social contribution.

What the third expression conveys is precisely this thought.

In the past Japanese style management, this thought was clearly stated.
However, it does not at all mean that Japanese style management has disregarded "profits."
Corporate executives under Japanese style management are also dedicated to the pursuit of profit, unsurprisingly.
But, the first and foremost purpose of their doing so is to support the living of their employees who give their best at work in order to feel the joy of contributing to society. Another purpose is to repay each shareholder who has believed in the company's future and has made an investment, and also to develop excellent products and services that realize happiness for many people in the world. And above all, they do so for the purpose of sustaining and further developing their wonderful company that contributes to society.
On the other hand, what leads executives under Japanese style management to think fully of profits is by no means the thought that it is the "ultimate purpose" of the company. In Japanese style management, the "ultimate purpose" is no doubt "to contribute to

society." Profits are a "means" for social contribution, not at all the "purpose."

This is precisely the "view of company" and the "view of profit" in Japanese style management and Japanese style capitalism.

However, in response to these statements above, readers may raise the following objection:

"No, that is not true. The purpose of a company and the duty of executives are definitely to maximize the company's profits as the representatives of shareholder's interests and then to return the profits to the shareholders. And also, a company and executives are to utilize the entrusted capital in the most efficient manner so as to grow the capital. This is the ultimate purpose of a company, the ultimate duty of executives, and the 'global standard' way of thinking."

For certain, this is an argument that we have constantly been hearing in these past few decades.

This also is an argument that many economists and business scholars worldwide have constantly been discussing.

However, to state frankly, this argument is also one that many executives as well as many workers in Japan have questioned deep down inside:

"That may be logically a valid argument. However, the management scene and the actual workplaces in Japanese companies are not operating under such logic. And, they cannot be operated that way."

Many people in Japan have thought in this manner about the argument.

Moreover, it is likely that even economists and business scholars who have been presenting this argument have secretly questioned their own logic.

However, it is not my intention to present an objection to this argument in this book.

It is not very meaningful to emotionally object to this argument.

It is also not productive to argue over the correctness of those two positions that essentially sit in two different paradigms.

Therefore, I would only like to present in this book the following two questions within the ground of the above argument:

What are the "shareholders' interests"?
And what is the "entrusted capital"?

What are the "shareholders' interests" that executives must increase as their duties?

And what is the "capital" that companies must increase as their purposes?

We need to give ourselves an opportunity to seriously think about these questions.

To start with, weren't problems such as the current subprime crisis and the collapse of GM caused by a mistake that corporate executives had made, where they crucially destroyed the "long-term shareholder profits" in the course of their hasty pursuit of increasing "short-term shareholder profits"?

Wasn't this a mistake where "invisible capital" such as trust capital, brand capital and culture capital were crucially destroyed in those executives' extreme pursuit of increasing the "visible capital" called "monetary capital"?

Weren't these mistakes a result of the way of corporate management whereby only "visible profits" and "visible capital" were considered, leaving "invisible profits" and "invisible capital" unconsidered?

These are the questions I would like to present here in this book.

In addition, these mistakes were not committed only within "corporate management."

Amid the storm of globalization, haven't many nations committed the same mistakes in their "management of state" as they constantly and earnestly pursue "economic growth" and "increase in GDP"?

It must be that we are now paying for the cost of those mistakes in the forms of global environmental problems as well as of social uncertainties caused by the widening gap between the rich and the poor.

The meaning of these matters will be further discussed in Chapter 12.

The Japanese Style Management

Which Has Already Embodied

"Social Enterprise"

Answers to these arguments "What are the purposes of companies?" and "What are the duties of executives?" are now being presented, not through engagement in "philosophical arguments" at a theoretical level, but rather through an actual movement of companies.

This is because a new vision for companies is being born at the leading edge of the world's capitalism, a form of companies that unifies "pursuit of profit" and "social contribution."

What is this?

It is "social enterprise."

That is, as the movements of CSR and social entrepreneurship spread throughout the world, the vision of "social enterprise" companies is now being born. These are not "for-profit companies" nor are they "non-profit organizations" in a simple sense, but ones that conduct activities for the purpose of contributing to society while working to gain necessary profits for independently sustaining their operations.

This vision of companies is very closely related to the earlier-mentioned "social entrepreneurship," a vision for professionals that start a new business for the purpose of social contribution. These two movements are just like two sides of the same coin.

However, when these new visions of "social enterprise" and "social entrepreneurship" are discussed, many people in Japan may feel a slight sense of surprise here once again.

That is because many Japanese workers actually believe that the ultimate purpose of companies is "social contribution," as mentioned earlier in the section where Japanese style management was discussed. It must be rather rare to find people in Japan who think of the company they work for as a "for-profit company whose ultimate purpose is to gain profits."

For instance, when company employees in Japan are asked, "What kind of company do you work for?" most of them will answer, "My company is one that contributes to society through such and such businesses," regardless of the type of company they work for.

Once, I was deeply impressed with the words by a Japanese corporate executive who appeared on a TV program as an interviewee.

This company, located in Tokyo, sells and delivers boxed lunches to customers working at the Otemachi and Marunouchi area, the very center of the Japanese economy. This executive stated in the interview that he always tells his employees, who are mostly younger people, the following words:

"The people you deliver these boxed lunches work at the Otemachi and Marunouchi area. They are the people who support

Japan. Delivering nutritious and tasty boxed lunches to them means you are supporting this country."

Any Japanese worker would be impressed and empathize with his words. Because, any Japanese person, regardless of the type of work he or she engage in, has or wishes to have a sense of pride in his or her job.

Behind this sense of pride is the earlier-mentioned "view of company" that is unique to the Japanese people.

That is, the view that "A company contributes to society through its main business."

In Japan, the notions of "for-profit companies that pursue profits" and "non-profit organizations that pursue social contribution" are not really perceived in a dichotomic sense.

Rather, the Japanese people have had the view of companies that incorporated far in advance the vision of "social enterprise," namely the vision that integrated the notions of "social contribution" and "pursuit of profit." The nation of Japan has already embodied the vision of "social enterprise" that the capitalism of the world is now starting to aim for.

In addition, behind this unique "view of company" has been another unique view by the Japanese people, that is, the unique "view of work."

As mentioned earlier, to work ("*hataraku*") in Japan literally means "for neighbors' happiness."

Thus, most Japanese people have had a sense that work is not merely "for earning their living" but "for the world and for the people."

However, in response to these statements above, readers who know the reality of Japan nowadays may oppose in this manner:

"That is just an idealistic theory. Today's Japan is filled with companies that are too busy thinking only of pursuing profits with no room for any consideration of social contribution. In addition, the reality is far from considering the joy of working because there are just so many workers who must focus only on surviving at their workplace, or rather, on working desperately in order to live."

I cannot object to this opinion.

I cannot deny the existence of this reality, either.

To be honest, I also have a mind to lament and criticize this reality of Japan together with those readers.

However, holding in the feeling, I would like to convey just this one thing here:

In Japanese companies, there used to be the wonderful view of company and the view of work, as well as wonderful corporate cultures.

And, we will certainly be able to bring back those wonderful ways of Japanese companies.

I only wish to convey this here.

Chapter 11

The Japanese Style Management
Which Has Pursued
the "Unification of Subject and Object"

The Age When the Spirit of
the "Unification of Subject and Object"
Is Required

Now, regarding "participatory economy" in the fourth paradigm shift.

What will be required when this new economy is being born?

Companies will be required to fundamentally change.

Because, "participatory economy" is, shortly speaking, an economy where there is no differentiation between companies and consumers.

For instance, the "prosumer communities" that are now spreading in the Internet world.

In these communities, consumers actively present their opinions on ideas and concepts of various products. They also exchange opinions freely with product developers of companies regarding improvement of existing products and development of new products. However, this relationship between consumers and companies is not a one-way relationship where, as in the conventional way, "companies hear consumers' opinions and incorporate them into improvements and developments of products." Consumers, in addition to expressing their needs, actively present opinions on how products can be improved. They freely present ideas on concepts of new products. They may at times present ideas on technical matters. Meanwhile, product developers of companies may at times express their views from a standpoint of a user and at other times may passionately express their thoughts as an engineer, pointing out technical issues in the ideas presented by consumers.

In other words, it can be said that in these communities there is no clear differentiation of who company employees are and who consumers are.

For another instance, the "affiliate" programs that have been spreading in the Internet world in recent years.

As discussed in Chapter 6, these are systems where consumers' opinions on what are appealing and excellent about their favorite products are shared on their own web sites or blogs which link to the sites where those introduced products can be purchased. When the visitors of those sites or blogs go through the links to the product purchase pages and purchase products, the consumers who shared the information about those products are rewarded benefit such as points.

In those affiliate programs, the hosting consumers are well acquainted with the attractiveness of those products, and concurrently, they in fact are well acquainted with the faults of the products. They may at times know more than the professionals of the company, and they may at times be able to talk about the appealing features in a more convincing manner than those professionals.

In other words, there is no differentiation of who marketing professionals of companies are and who consumers are in this instance as well. This is also the case with the "group purchase," a system in which consumers solicit each other on the Internet to co-purchase a product with a good number of people. There is no differentiation of who sales professionals of companies are and who consumers are.

As illustrated above, "participatory economy" is, in a sense, an economy where there is no differentiation between companies and consumers.

If so, when this "participatory economy" emerges and expands, what will be required of companies?

The "Illness of Operationalism"

Which Is Affecting Many Companies Today

As a matter of fact, there is one greatly important matter that will be required of companies owing to the emergence of this new economy.

It is actually an extremely important matter.

To abandon "operationalism."

That is what will be required of companies.

That is, the "idea of manipulating consumers to move in the direction of what the company wishes."

Companies will need to abandon this idea.

This statement may surprise some readers, but in reality at the present time, a number of companies have unconsciously fallen into this "operationalism." However, since many companies are unconscious about it, they do not realize the fact that they are falling into the idea. They are not aware of what they are doing.

Then, what is "operationalism"?

This can be comprehended well when we look into the words that people casually use in their daily operation of companies:

"What can we do to get customers to turn to this product?"
"How can we get customers to buy this?"
"What can we do to get consumers to become repeat customers?"
"How can we get customers to become the fans of our company?"

People must be constantly using these words.

Of course, it is not that these words are used through ill intentions.

However, we need to become aware of this "unconscious operationalism" that is hidden behind these words. Because, it is this unconsciousness that is causing the relationship between companies and consumers to be rather empty with no sympathy between each other in today's markets of capitalism.

Moreover, this "operationalism" is not a problem that only companies are falling into.

"Operationalism" should be referred to as a "modern illness" by which many people in the world are affected. We will be able to see this well if we, for instance, go to a bookstore and look at the titles of an array of books that are on display.

"Techniques to See into Others' Minds"
"How to Motivate Your Employees"
"Speeches to Convince Your Customers"
"How to Convince Others"

That is, we have unconscious desire to "manipulate others as we wish" deep down inside. And the world is flooded with books that stimulate this sort of desire.

Then, why is this "illness of operationalism" epidemic in the modern world?

One of the reasons must be that many people are stirred by the words "survival" and "being the winner" amid the extremely severe storm of "principles of competition" in modern capitalism. It must be that, as a result, many people are unconsciously influenced by a simplistic idea of considering surrounding people—subordinates, employees, customers, and vendors—to be "tools" or "machines" and to efficiently manipulate them for promptly accomplishing their objectives.

In addition, there is another profound reason behind this.

It is the "mechanical system paradigm," which was discussed in Chapter 3.

That is, as we entered the 20th century and experienced the rapid growth of science and technology, the machine civilization blossomed dynamically and enabled our lives to be extremely convenient. Due to various equipment produced by the machine civilization, such as automobiles, airplanes, telephones, the Internet, TV sets, refrigerators, air conditioners, washing machines and so forth, our lives have become extremely convenient.

However, the overwhelming success of this machine civilization caused an unconscious illusion to bud in many people's minds. That is, the illusion that what are in front of them are machines and that it is possible to freely and adeptly manipulate them by scientifically analyzing their mechanism.

This illusion has pervaded almost every field. For instance, new engineering disciplines such as "sense engineering" and "attractiveness engineering" have been created to analyze even such things as human feelings and what attract humans. In the management of companies, the field of management engineering has been created, where they analyze company organizations by treating them as mechanical systems, and thus the terms "reengineering" and "restructuring" have been coined.

This "illness of operationalism" is quite deep-rooted, and it has penetrated even into expressions that we casually use through good intentions.

For instance, the word "motivation."

We often and casually use such an expression as "improve motivation of employees," but at the basis of this expression actually lies the idea of operationalism, the idea of manipulating staff and employees top-down and getting them to feel motivated so that a higher productivity can be achieved. And it is this unconsciousness of executives and managers that is causing the relationship between the management and the employees in business operations to be, here again, rather empty with no sympathy between each other.

We should realize the dreadfulness of this situation.

This operationalism, that is, a "modern illness," is directly reflected also in the way that companies think of customers and consumers.

Operationalism takes effect starting with this idea: "How can we get customers to buy our company's products?"

Based on this operationalism, companies utilize massive amounts of advertisement and clever sales promotions to forcefully stimulate the buying motive of consumers to get them to purchase the company's products. Then this operationalism further expands.

It expands to the stage where they think "How can we lead customers to replace old products with new products?" and then it escalates to "How can we get them to throw away their usable products and to purchase new products instead?"

Thus, the "company-centric" way of thinking becomes more dominant, where companies not only get consumers to purchase the companies' products but also get consumers to throw away usable goods so that they will purchase new products from the companies.

What is happening here?

"Stimulating people's desire for consumption and their buying motive will lead to company profits."

When this desire-promoting thought and the idea of operationalism meet with each other, capitalism comes to bring about the worst problems.

One of the symbolic cases of this is, needless to say, the "global environmental problems."

As a result of intensified human desire as well as mass production and mass consumption, the destruction of the global environment was brought about.

Another symbolic case of the worst problems caused by the operationalism of companies is the "subprime crisis" that has brought about the current global economic crisis.

Similarly with the idea of "How can we get customers to throw away their usable products and to purchase new products instead?", "subprime crisis" was caused by the worst idea of operationalism.

That is, the idea of "How can we get people to buy products that they cannot afford?"

Wasn't it this idea that produced subprime mortgage lending for lower-income groups?

That is, with this idea of operationalism, companies thought about intentionally manipulating consumers to get them to purchase what they could not afford, so that the companies would gain profits. Wasn't it this idea of operationalism that brought about the subprime crisis and misled capitalism worldwide?

The "View of Customer"

in Japanese Style Management

However, within the new economic paradigm of "participatory economy," this "operationalism" of companies will be severely criticized by consumers.

This is because "participatory economy" is an economy where companies and consumers work together on developing and improving products, and where consumers voluntarily promote, sell and purchase products. Therefore, if companies in conducting these activities have the thought of private gains to "make use of customers' wisdom" or a calculation to "make use of customers' ability to promote sales of products," the consumers in the coming age will keenly sense the companies' calculative way of thinking and will see through their idea of "operationalism."

Then, where does this "operationalism" emerge in the first place?

As a matter of fact, it emerges from the perception that companies and consumers are on opposing sides.

In this perception, the feelings of "empathy," "gratitude" and "unity" that should surely be born between companies and customers are disregarded, and companies and customers are considered to be opposing sides as the "products sellers" and the "product purchasers." And furthermore, companies think of customers as the "objects of manipulation."

This is where "operationalism" originates.

This way of thinking has penetrated even into the recently-prevalent term "customer satisfaction." The argument of how companies can enhance "customer satisfaction" through perceiving customers as the objects of that "customer satisfaction," seems on the surface to be based on good intentions, but it is secretly penetrated by the idea that cuts off the relationship between companies and customers psychologically. This fact is clear when we imagine this one situation:

In the old days, was there ever an excellent salesperson or businessperson who visited customers for business meetings and thought "Now, let's gain customer satisfaction. Let's improve customer satisfaction."?

The answer is, no.

People who have experienced the preciousness of heart-to-heart exchanges and empathy with customers in the actual business world must have felt that something was wrong with this argument of customer satisfaction.

Along with the argument of "motivation," the argument of "customer satisfaction" seems to be a reasonable one at first, but it must have been created by the "stealthy operationalism" where customers and consumers are viewed as the "objects" of efforts to enhance the "degree of satisfaction."

To start with, ever since the idea of business first emerged, have there been businesses that do not think of "customer satisfaction"? If a business is an honest one, hasn't the idea of "customers being satisfied" been just so natural that it should not even be argued?

The fact itself that the argument mentioned above is plausibly engaged reflects the "illness" of current capitalism. We should realize this condition.

Wasn't the term "customer satisfaction" created due to the reality that in current capitalism we have been oblivious to the starting point of businesses, have fallen into extreme pursuit of profits, and have forgotten how precious it is that customers are happy?

However, when discussing this issue, we may realize that the value systems required by this new economy called "participatory economy" are also the value systems which used to be emphasized in the past Japanese style management.

Why is it?

In Japanese style management, the perception originally did not exist where companies and consumers are on opposing sides.

Because, underneath Japanese style management lies the national culture of Japan whose essence is expressed in the following term:

"The unification of subject and object."

That is the term.

The utmost wisdom of Japanese culture has been the "unification of self and others" and the "unification of host (subject) and guest (object)," where people do not perceive self and others as existing separately. Therefore, in Japanese style management as well, companies and customers were originally perceived as a unified whole.

What symbolize this fact are the following words that have long been mentioned in workplaces in Japanese companies:

"Customers are the mirrors that reflect our minds."

As symbolized in these words, in Japanese companies, executives and employees originally did not have the idea of perceiving "customers" as "objects to sell products to." "Customers" were considered to be valued people who corporate executives and employees encountered through the "*enishi*"(destined relationship) of product purchase and sale, and thus they were able to look at themselves in the "mirrors" called customers through which they humbly received the opportunities for growth.

This spirit used to exist in the operations of Japanese companies.

This was reflected in such expressions and a sense of value as "We have been nurtured by customers" and "We grow together with our customers."

And there is more. Not only this "view of customer" in Japanese companies was connected to the thought of the "unification of host and guest," it was also connected to the thought of "sincere hospitality" and the spirit expressed as "Treasure every encounter, for it will never recur." These thoughts are the essence of the Japanese culture, forming extremely profound thoughts that could sometimes be viewed to be religious.

In the coming age when "participatory economy" expands, companies must abandon operationalism toward their customers and instead value the empathy for and the unity with customers. In such an age, the "view of customer" in Japanese style management should be revalued, along with the spirit, thoughts and cultures that stand behind the view.

And it will be extremely important in the coming age to deeply consider the spirit, thoughts and cultures that are at the basis of Japanese style management, in order to think about which path the nation of Japan should take.

For instance, "*mono-zukuri*" (making things) that has been considered the strength of Japan.

This strength is actually not just about techniques and ability that support "making things."

The strength of Japan's "*mono-zukuri*" in fact is the strength of the spirit, thoughts and cultures where people put "heart" into "making things." We should realize this fact.

For instance, people in Japan hold a deep spirit to consider one product as a "work of art," not just "merchandise." They have a mature culture where they put "heart" into the "things" they make.

When we recognize the profoundness of the spirit, thoughts and culture of Japan, we will come to see more clearly what role Japan should be taking in the paradigm shift to "global environment economy," which is to be discussed in the next chapter, as well as what the strength of Japanese style management is.

Chapter 12

The Japanese Style Management Which Has Assumed "*Yugen*" (Limitedness), "*Mujo*" (Impermanence) and "*Jinen*" (Living as Nature)

The Spirit of "*Yugen*," "*Mujo*" and "*Jinen*" Which the World Can Learn

Finally, regarding the fifth paradigm shift.
It is the paradigm shift from "unlimited growth economy" to "global environment economy."

As discussed in Chapter 7, this paradigm shift means that, as the global environmental problems become more serious, economies need shifts from assuming "unlimited space," "unlimited resource" and "unlimited growth" to assuming "limited space," "limited resource" and "limited growth."

Then, why will the value systems of Japan be important in this economic paradigm shift?
The reason for this is clear.

It is because the various problems confronting the current world are of the kinds that Japan has been faced with since very far back in time.

That is, the entire human society is currently faced with the "limitedness" in various issues such as global environment, resources and energy, but in fact the nation of Japan has always assumed "limited space" and "limited resources" since the very old days and has accordingly realized economic growth.

Behind this fact is the reality that Japan has basically been a smaller-sized island nation, that it experienced more than two centuries of isolation policy from early 1600s to the mid 1800s in the Edo period, and that with the exception of a period of time preceding and during the Second World War it did not attempt to colonize other lands to secure larger territory and more resources. Due to this background, Japan has assumed "small homeland" and "limited resources" since the old days and has accordingly realized economic growth as well as cultivated a mature culture.

This is symbolized by the fact that the nation had already realized, by a certain point in time in the Edo period, the world's leading technologies for recycling and environmental protection as well as the most advanced urban technologies. The culture of emphasizing these matters has been passed down as the "culture of conciseness" and the "spirit of *Mottainai*" (considering resources as precious and reusing them by using wisdom), which has contributed to the flowering of leading edge "space-saving," "energy-saving" and "resource-saving" technologies in the nation.

In other words, in Japan, the "culture that assumes limitedness" has been strongly tied to the "technologies that assume limitedness."

And, in the coming age, it is extremely important to understand this fact when considering the path Japan should take.

Because, when we discuss what the strength of Japan is, we tend to focus only on the "strength of its technologies." However, the strength of Japan in the environmental field is not at all limited to "technologies." Rather, it is the nation's mature "thoughts" and "culture" which firmly exist at the basis of those "technologies" that Japan should proudly present to the world.

When we understand this fact, we then realize that what Japan should offer to the world in the field of "environmental technologies" is not only the technologies themselves but is actually the combination of "environmental technologies, environmental thoughts, and environmental culture."

For instance, when Japan offers technologies for resource recycling to the world, it should concurrently offer the Japanese thought of "*Mottainai*," the spirit of considering resources as precious and reusing them by using wisdom, which the Nobel Peace Prize winner Wangari Maathai has been working to promote to the world. When the nation offers technologies for forestry conservation, it should do so along with the Japanese culture of viewing that "The forest is inhabited by something sacred."

However, in response to these statements, some readers may present the following question:

"But isn't it the technologies of Japan after all that the world wants, and isn't it the technologies themselves that sell as products?"

In response to this question, I would like to ask the following question:

Now in the age when the entire globe is faced with the environmental problems, what should Japan think of? Is it "expanding exports" as a nation, or "contributing to the world" through helping to resolve the global environmental problems?

If the answer is the latter, the path that Japan should choose is obvious.

Japan should not simply offer "technologies" as "products"; what it should offer to the world is the combination of "technologies, thoughts and culture" as a "way of society" for this age when we are faced with the global environmental problems.

And the importance of this does not apply only to the field of "environment."

For instance, in the field of "aging societies" as well, Japan can offer various technologies required by the world, such as medical devices for home use, barrier-free furniture, and special equipments for elderly care. Japan should not simply aim for exporting these "technologies," but it should offer them along with the nation's "spirit of caring for others," the "culture of helping each other," and the "thought of terminal care" (respecting the dignity of persons passing away and watching over their last moments).

This strength that Japan can offer is the same in the field of "*mono-zukuri*" (making things), as discussed in Chapter 11, and is even more applicable in the field of "services" that do not involve making "things."

Because, the "service industry" in today's Japan is so fully equipped with written manuals and advanced information systems that it has left behind the excellent Japanese spirit, thoughts and culture.

The service industry in Japan has its roots in such wonderful traditions as the "spirit of treasuring every encounter," the "thought of the unification of host and guest," and the "culture of sincere hospitality." If so, what Japan should do is to revive the way of service industry that is based on these wonderful spirit, thoughts and culture, and this wonderful way is what Japan should present to the world.

Then, why am I presenting this view?

Why will Japan need to present to the world these profound spirit, thoughts and culture?

I mentioned the reason for this earlier.

It is because the various problems confronting the world are of the kinds that Japan has been faced with since very far back in time.

And through experiencing those problems in the course of its long history, Japan has been cultivating the spirit, thoughts and culture that the world can learn now.

As a matter of fact, this does not apply only to the dimension of "businesses."

At the dimensions of "culture" and "civilization" as well, the nation of Japan, oddly enough, has long been learning the "new value systems" that the entire human society will be learning from now.

The Culture of "Japan" Which Has Reflected the Future of the World

Then, what are those "new value systems"?

As we are faced with various global-scale problems such as the environmental problems, the economic crisis and widespread terrorism, human society is entering the age when it should shift its basic value systems.

This shift should be referred to as the "five shifts in value systems" as described below.

The first is the shift from "unlimitedness" to "limitedness."

This was discussed earlier.

The strong-rooted desire for "unlimitedness" existing in the human society centered around developed nations. And also, the illusion of "unlimited growth." Now that the assumption of "unlimitedness" has hit a wall, human society should accept the reality of "limitedness" and shift its value systems to those that assume "limited growth."

However, in this age when we need to shift our value systems, we may realize the fact that Japan actually has already been long cultivating the value systems that assume "limitedness."

The second is the shift from "permanence" to "impermanence."

In the value systems up to the present which have been centered around the United States, people have had the illusion and desire that the entire world is unified with a single value and that this condition will permanently continue, as symbolized in the term "global standards." Meanwhile, as symbolized in the words "dog years," the world in reality has entered the age when changes happen dramatically and values change in a dizzying pace.

However, despite the fact that the world has just entered the age when values change rapidly, Japan has long been cultivating the culture based on the thought of "*mujo*" (impermanence), namely, the culture that is prepared for the transience of every existence. This culture shares roots with the national character of Japan that is marked by the love for cherry blossoms which bloom all at once and then drop all at once within the same season. And, behind the "view of impermanence" of the Japanese people is the deep spirit through which they believe in the "things that continue to exist even in the changes." In other words, behind the "view of impermanence" is the deep spirit of believing in "eternity".

The third is the shift from "conquering nature" to "living as nature."

In Western societies, "nature" has basically been a target of "conquest." Therefore, attempts have been made in the Western world to remake nature accordingly to human wishes by scientifically analyzing its mechanism and with the technologies developed by utilizing the knowledge thus acquired. However, this kind of value system has now hit a wall through the serious problem of the global warming. We have now realized that we do not have the ability to even control the temperature in the Earth's environment. Thus, the view of nature as "a target of conquest" is being forced to change. This is why people throughout the world today talk about "living with nature."

However, in Japanese history, the idea or value of viewing nature as a target of "conquest" has never been dominant. Rather, to Japanese people, nature has been a "great existence" that gives life to humans and that has been viewed as something sacred which should never be violated. Behind this Japanese view of nature has been a religious sentiment that considers everything in this world to contain the Buddha nature, as symbolized in the words found in Buddhist thought: "In mountains, rivers, grass, trees, lands: everywhere resides the Buddha nature, no matter where."

And, what people in Japan have placed the most value on is, not accomplishing something by "artificial" forces, but the state of "*jinen*" (living as nature) that is naturally accomplished through being lead by this "great existence." At the root of this "*jinen*" thought are once again the thought of the "unification of self and others" and the "unification of subject and object" in which people perceive themselves and the world they live in as a unified whole. And, when taking the viewpoint of the "unification of self and others," the thought of "living with nature" that people around the world talk about today is not quite adequate. Because, although the thought of "living with nature" is more profound by quite a degree than the thought of "conquest," it is still based on the "separation of self and others." The thought is still inadequate in the sense that nature is perceived as existing separately from humans and that humans only seek to co-exist and live with nature. Thus, the "view of nature" of the Japanese people is an extremely profound one as symbolized in the word "*jinen*" which means "living as nature" beyond simply "living with nature."

The fourth is the shift from "exclusion" to "inclusion."

146

In the world up to the present, there have been different ideologies in conflict, and people who differ in ideologies have been competing against each other as they insist on the correctness of their thoughts. There was once an ideological conflict between "capitalism" and "socialism," and after the Cold War between the East and the West came the civilizational conflict between "Christianity" and "Islamism." Conflicts of these kinds brought about the threat for a catastrophic nuclear war in the past, and they are now causing unending threat for terrorism.

Taking the viewpoint to reflect on the unproductive situations caused by these "conflicts," the importance of "pluralistic value" is now being discussed. "Pluralistic value" is the idea that various values co-exist in an environment of mutual respect, without controlling the world with "monistic value" where only one value is considered absolute.

However, Japan is a nation wherein this "pluralistic value" has actually been embodied since the old days. Because, unlike "monotheistic" religions of Western and Islamic nations, the indigenous religions of Japan are essentially "polytheistic" and, prior to the emergence of "polytheism," they were based on "animism" where gods and the Buddha nature are considered to dwell within every existence in the world. This view is symbolized by the following facts: In the Japanese indigenous religion Shinto, the notion of "multitudinous gods" is referred; in the Japanese Buddhism, the thought of "Mahayana" which includes every existence in the world is referred; there existed the thoughts wherein Shinto and Buddhism are integrated into one, such as "*honji-suijaku*" (the thought wherein the gods of Shinto are considered to be various forms of manifestation of Buddha) and "*shinbutsu-shugo*"(the unification of Shinto gods and Buddha).

The fifth is the shift from "efficiency" to "meaning."

The world up to now, centered around developed nations, has considered "economic growth" to be the absolute proposition, and therefore the world has been in a rush under the notion that "efficiency" is of the highest value, seeking to be as "fast," as "large in quantity" and as "easy" as possible.

However, as we are faced with the global environmental problems and the global economic crisis, the sense of value to focus only on "efficiency" is now being reflected on throughout the world. Additionally, the world is starting to recognize the preciousness of discovering the "meanings" in various things by the value measures different from the measure of "efficiency." This way of recognizing values is demonstrated in such forms as the advocacy of "slow life" and of "LOHAS" (Lifestyles of Health and Sustainability).

However, in Japan, "efficiency" has never been considered to be of the highest value. There never existed a culture in Japan where "being fast," "being large in quantity" or "having an easy way" are considered to be the absolute values. This fact is symbolized by the existence of the various expressions that people in Japan have respected: "When in a hurry, take a longer route," "Great talents mature late," "He is rich that has few wants," "Light up a small corner of society," "Good can come out of a misfortune," and "There are difficulty and easiness in life." The Japanese are basically a people who find values in "walking slow" at times, sense the truth in "something small," and discover profound meanings in the "bitterness of life."

As seen above, in this age when we are faced with various global-scale problems, such as the environmental problems, the economic crisis and widespread terrorism, human society is moving toward these "five shifts in value systems." However, these "new value systems" that human society is starting to learn are, oddly enough, "nostalgic value systems" that Japan has respected since far back in time. And this sense of values certainly exists at the deep core of such things as Japanese style management and Japanese style capitalism.

We should first realize this fact.

And, if we realize this fact, then we will be able to understand:
In the coming age, why will Japanese style management and
Japanese style capitalism revive?
We will be able to understand the deepest reason for this.

Chapter 13

Why Will Japanese Style Management Revive?

Japanese Style Management

Will Revive with "New Values"

Why will Japanese style management revive?
Why will Japanese style capitalism revive?

The deepest reason for this is that in the coming age the economic principles will achieve fundamental paradigm shifts and therefore capitalism itself will greatly evolve. It is also because the "new value systems" which will be required as a result of this evolution are in fact "nostalgic value systems" that used to be considered important in Japanese style management and that existed at the basis of Japanese style capitalism.

However, I am not referring to this matter through a mere "nostalgia for the good old days."
"In the olden days, Japanese style management was great."
"In the olden days, Japanese style capitalism was great."
It is not through this kind of "retrospective thinking" that I am referring to this matter.

Now, please remember once again what was discussed in Chapter 2.

What we are about to experience is the "dialectic of history" and the "spiral development of capitalism."

Therefore, the events that will happen from now are not merely "the revivals of old things."
They will be the revivals of "old and nostalgic things" that are accompanied by "new values."

This is also the case in the revivals of Japanese style management and Japanese style capitalism.
When the Japanese style management and the Japanese style capitalism of the past revive, they will invariably revive accompanied by "new values."
This is what we should deeply consider.

Then what are those "new values"?

We should keep the following two perspectives.

The first is that the revivals will be accompanied by "rationalization."
When Japanese style management and Japanese style capitalism revive from now, they will not necessarily be accompanied by "old and conventional elements" or "impractical and inefficient elements" that existed in the past. They will revive in the forms that have incorporated "modern elements" and "practical and efficient elements" of Western style management and Western style capitalism.
For instance, in mature knowledge societies from now, sharing "tacit knowing" and "wisdom inexpressive in words" will become important, so the nostalgic Japanese way of "master-and-apprentice" relationship will likely revive in workplaces. However, this revival will not necessarily be accompanied by the element of the "conventional apprentice system" that demanded the obedience of apprentices.

The second is that the revivals will be accompanied by "updates."

When Japanese style management and Japanese style capitalism revive from now, they will revive incorporating the latest movements of information revolution and capitalism. Especially, new business processes that utilize information technologies and new business models that utilize the Internet. Those will be incorporated into the revivals.

For instance, what symbolizes this fact is the "Net shops" in Japan. Many of the popular "Net shops" in Japan that are achieving high sales are actually those that value the "spirit of sincere hospitality" and "empathy for and unity with customers." The Internet businesses are also achieving evolution as they merge with Japanese style management.

As described above, what is about to occur now is not the simple revivals of Japanese style management and Japanese style capitalism. What is about to occur now is "spiral development." And, the essence of "spiral development" is that the "evolution to the future" and the "regression to the origin" occur simultaneously.

In other words, in Japanese style management and Japanese style capitalism, the "evolution to the future" and the "regression to the origin" are concurrently about to occur.

Then, is this a movement unique to Japan?
Not so.

If the movement follows the law of spiral development in dialectic, "old and nostalgic values" will invariably revive accompanied by "new values," both in the management and in the capitalism of the West.

And, this movement has already started.

The Age When the Nation of Japan

Contributes to the World

Then, what are those "old and nostalgic values"?
What are those "old and nostalgic values" that will revive?

They are, "invisible values."
"Invisible values" that we have lost sight of amid the
overwhelming dominance of "monetary economy" will revive not
only within Japan but also in the developed capitalist nations of the
world.

However, when these revivals happen, we should not forget this:
There will be an important roll for the nation of Japan to assume.
Because, Japan has been nurturing the "culture of discovering
values in invisible things" in the course of its long history and
tradition, and this culture is something that the entire world can
learn from.
However, I am not referring to this matter through "the
mentality of nationalism."
"After all, Japan is great."
"After all, Japan is who leads the world."
It is not through this kind of narrow-minded nationalism that I
refer to this matter.

What I have in mind is just this one thought:

In the 21st century, in what ways can Japan contribute to the
world?

This is the thought I have in mind.

In the past, Japan went through a period of time when it displayed its overwhelming "power" in monetary economy. In those days, Japan intended to contribute to the world through exercising "economic power," but the bursting of the economic bubble in the late 1980s put an end to this dream-like party of spending.

Then, in the coming age, how can Japan as a nation contribute to the world?

I venture to say what I have in mind.

The "power of mature culture."

Shouldn't Japan contribute to the world by utilizing this power?

If the nation stops looking at other nations far beyond its surrounding oceans with admiration and envy, and if it turns its eyes to the ground on which it stands, there actually is a rich soil that has cultivated the nation's wonderful history, culture, thoughts, spirit, and the senses of values and aesthetics.

What we Japanese should deeply consider is the ground, and its soil.

And, when we realize the existence of the rich ground and the soil, that will be the beginning.

The beginning of the rebirth of Japan.
And, the beginning of Japan's contribution to the world.

That is, the contribution through the nation's "power of mature culture."

However, the meaning of this is not simply to "export culture."
It is not simply to introduce Japanese arts, music, literature, *haiku* poetry, handicrafts and various forms of entertainment to the world.

Then, what is it?

The evolution of "corporate management" through mature culture.
And the evolution of "capitalism" through mature culture.

It is about leading these evolutions.
It is about leading the world in realizing these evolutions.
If Japan is to realize this, it will be a wonderful contribution to the world, beyond simply "exporting culture."

And, I have already mentioned the meaning of "mature culture."

A culture that discovers values in invisible things.

If so, what should we all be aiming for?

"Corporate management that considers invisible values."
"Capitalism that emphasizes invisible capital."

Therefore, I have named this book:

"Invisible Capitalism."

Now in the midst of the global economic crisis, what is it that we should be seeking?

We should find out the vision of the evolution of capitalism that will come beyond these winter years.

However, we will not be able to see this vision only by looking into the "future."

In fact, through looking back over our "past,"
and through looking back over our "origin,"

we will be able to see it.

Because, in the history we live,
the "evolution to the future" and the "regression to the origin"
occur simultaneously.
What teaches us this is the Dialectic of Hegel.

"The law of spiral development."

And, if the world is to develop as if
it were climbing a spiral staircase,
what we should be aiming for is obvious:

The nation of Japan,
should be strongly and steadily
climbing up the spiral staircase,
leading the world toward the summit.

The Five Paradigm Shifts Which Will Occur in the Economic Principle of Capitalism

---

The first paradigm shift:
from "Operationalism Economy"
to "Complexity Economy"

The second paradigm shift:
from "Knowledge Economy"
to "Empathy Economy"

The third paradigm shift:
from "Monetary Economy"
to "Voluntary Economy"

The fourth paradigm shift:
from "Beneficiary Economy"
to "Participatory Economy"

The fifth paradigm shift:
from "Unlimited Growth Economy"
to "Global Environment Economy"

Acknowledgements

First, I would like to express my sincere appreciation to Mr. Jorge Pinto for editing and publishing this English version of my book. Without the destined encounter (*Deep Enishi*) with Mr. Pinto, this book could not have come into the world.

And I would like to express my deep gratitude to Mr. Hisao Nishimiya, a translation coordinator, Ms. Kiyoe Parisien, a translator, and Mr. Tomoki Hotta of Babel Corporation for their dedicated cooperation in the translation of this book.

I would also like to thank Ms. Kumi Fujisawa, a co-founder of Think Tank SophiaBank. This book was born with the support of her advice. Her frank opinions as the first reader always provide me with the strength for the final revision.

I would also like to give deep thanks to my family, Sumiko, Sayer and Yue, for their watching warmly over me writing this book. Before I knew it, each of my family members has come to work on their own pieces of art, design and music.

In this early summer, pleasant breeze is being sent from Mt. Fuji, and as I stroll, birds are filling the forest with their music as they rejoice this wonderful season.

Looking up at Mt. Fuji, which tranquilly and majestically stands before the clear blue sky, I feel that the invisible future far away can be seen.

Lastly, I would like to dedicate this book to my father and mother who are not with us anymore. Even during their most difficult times they always turned their eyes to the future.
And their deep eyes are what gave life to this book.

Hiroshi Tasaka
June 2, 2009

Profile of the Author

Hiroshi Tasaka graduated from the Faculty of Engineering at the University of Tokyo with a Ph.D. in nuclear engineering in 1981.

From 1987, he worked as a visiting researcher at the Battelle Memorial Institute and also at the Pacific Northwest National Laboratories in the USA.

In 1990, he participated in founding the Japan Research Institute and engaged in "Industry Incubation" as a Chief Strategy Officer.

In 2000, he became a Professor at the Graduate School of Tama University in Tokyo and teaches students the philosophy, vision, policy, strategy, skills, mind and spirit of social entrepreneur and social enterprise.

Also in 2000, he founded Think Tank SophiaBank, a "Paradigm Think Tank" whose mission is to change the "paradigms of social systems" in human society to solve the "global problems" and "frontier problems" for the society. In order to achieve this mission, SophiaBank formed a worldwide network that connects social entrepreneurs and acts as a "Socio-Incubator" that encourages social entrepreneurs to change old paradigms and to create new social systems.

In 2003, he established the Japan Social Entrepreneur Forum (JSEF) under SophiaBank to foster and support social entrepreneurs in order to bring about innovation and change in global society.

In 2006, he was nominated as a member of "US-Japan Innovators" by the Japan Society in New York.

Also, he was invited as a member of the Global Agenda Council of the World Economic Forum (Davos Conference) in 2008.

Tasaka is a philosopher who has put forward a wide range of ideas and theories: philosophies of life and work, thoughts of business and management, strategies of industry and corporate, policies of society and government, visions of the Internet revolution and the knowledge society, and also paradigm changes of global society.

He is the author of more than 50 books, including
The Age of Paradigm Shift;
The Five Laws to Foresee the Future;
Wisdom of Complexity;
The Gaia Perspective;
Ecology of Mind;
What Will Happen in the Knowledge Society?;
A New Paradigm of Strategic Thinking;
Management of Complex Systems;
Management of Tacit Knowing;
The Evolution of the Professional;
The Philosophy of Work;
Why Do We Work?;
What Is the Reward of Working?;
What Is Success in Life?; and
To the Summit
—Why Should You Embrace an Ideal in Your Heart?.

tasaka@hiroshitasaka.jp
http://www.hiroshitasaka.jp/
http://www.sophiabank.co.jp/

www.ingramcontent.com/pod-product-compliance
Lightning Source LLC
Chambersburg PA
CBHW031810190326
41518CB00006B/275